Contents

Level Two

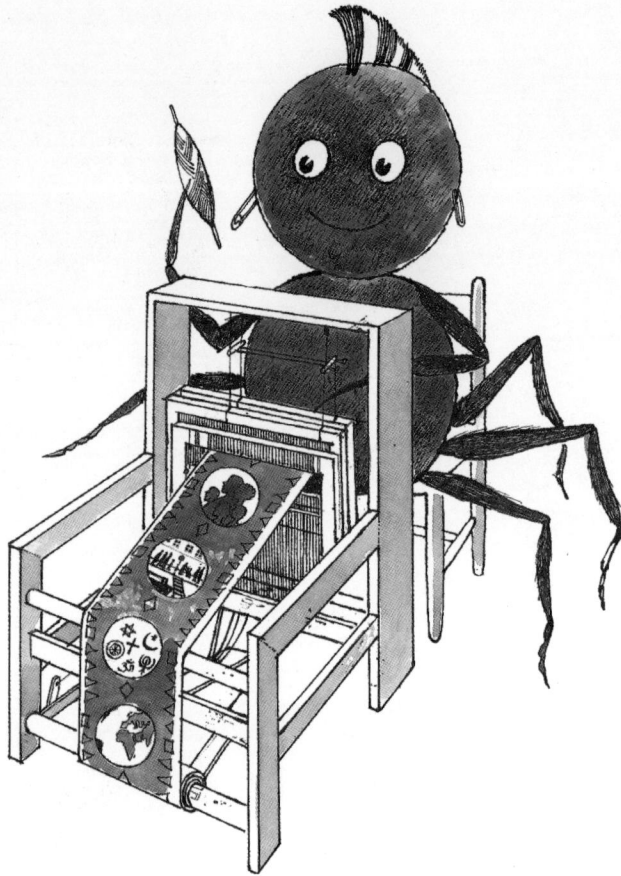

This is the start of the work you will be doing in Level Two of this course called

WEAVING THE WEB

If you have completed Level One of this course you will recall that as a spider criss-crosses strands to make a web, or a weaver works strands of thread together to make a pattern, this course also weaves a picture of how people make sense of life, especially in the major world religions.

> If you have completed Level One,
> - *recall three tasks which you enjoyed doing.*
> - *talk about any display work you produced.*

If *Weaving the Web* is a new religious education programme for you, then

WELCOME

> *Write three sentences about the kind of religious education you have done before.*

This programme is arranged in units of work called modules. Each module has tasks for you to do. Part of your work will include self-assessment tasks where you will assess how your work has gone. These tasks are part of your learning. There are three modules in this book: Communication, Celebration and Values. Each of these titles deals with learning about a very important aspect of life.

Communication

Celebration

Values

Weaving the Web

Communication
Celebration·Values

Level 2

A modular programme of Religious Education

Richard Lohan and Mary McClure SND

Collins

Collins Liturgical Publications
8 Grafton Street, London W1X 3LA

Collins Liturgical in Canada
Novalis, Box 9700, Terminal
375 Rideau St, Ottawa, Ontario K1G 4B4

Collins Dove
PO Box 316, Blackburn, Victoria 3130

Collins Liturgical New Zealand
PO Box 1, Auckland

First published 1989
© 1989 Richard Lohan and Mary McClure

Programme Components
Community, Story, People

Level One	0 00 599149 8
Level Two	0 00 599150 1
Level Three	0 00 599151 X

Communication, Celebration, Values

Level One	0 00 599152 8
Level Two	0 00 599153 6
Level Three	0 00 599154 4

Teacher's Book	0 00 599156 0

The National Project of Catechesis and Religious
Education
Published with the authority of the Department for
Christian Doctrine and Formation of the Bishop's
Conference of England and Wales

Nihil obstat Father Anton Cowan, *censor*
Imprimatur Rt. Rev. John Crowley, V.G., Bishop in Central London
Westminster, 8th May, 1989
The Nihil obstat and Imprimatur are a declaration that a book or pamphlet
is considered to be free from doctrinal or moral error. It is not implied
that those who have granted the Nihil obstat and Imprimatur agree with
the contents, opinions or statements expressed.

Acknowledgements

p. 11: *Prayer before retiring to rest at night*,
reproduced from the Authorised Prayer Book of the
United Hebrew Congregations of the British
Commonwealth of Nations with permission of the
Singer's Prayer Book Publication Committee;
pp. 17, 47: extracts from the English translation of
The Roman Missal © 1973, ICEL, and
p. 47: extracts from the English translation of the
Rite of Holy Week © 1970, ICEL. All rights
reserved; p. 41: extracts from *A Passover Haggada*,
Central Conference of American Rabbis © Penguin
Books USA Inc.; p. 44: extract from the *Jerusalem
Bible*, published and copyright 1966, 1967 and 1968
by Darton, Longman and Todd Ltd and Doubleday
& Co. Inc., and is used by permission of the
publishers; p. 71: extracts of declarations on religion
and nature made at WWF's 25th anniversary
celebrations in Assisi, Italy in September 1986.
cover photo: Andes Press Agency
photo credits: p. 2: Andes Press Agency; p. 5: Andes
Press Agency; p. 8: Andes Press Agency;
p. 11: David Richardson; p. 13: Andes Press
Agency; p. 14: (left) Andes Press Agency; (right)
David Richardson; p. 17: Andes Press Agency;
p. 18: Mary Evans Picture Library; p. 20: (top)
Bellarmine College Library; (bottom) Samye-Ling
Tibetan Centre; Andes Press Agency; p. 21: (top)
Andes Press Agency; (bottom) Camera Press;
p. 29: Andes Press Agency; p. 32: Mary Evans
Picture Library; p. 33: Andes Press Agency;
p. 34: Rex Features; Brenda Prince; Andes Press
Agency; Rex Features; Andes Press Agency; Andes
Press Agency; Brenda Prince; p. 36: (top) Andes
Press Agency; (bottom) Rex Features; p. 39: Frank
Spooner Pictures; p. 41: David Richardson;
p. 43: Hutchison Library; Hutchison Library;
Popperfoto; p. 46: (top left clockwise) Andes Press
Agency; Andes Press Agency; Anne King; Andes
Press Agency; Andes Press Agency; (middle)
Anne King; p. 48: Andes Press Agency; p. 60: Sally
& Richard Greenhill; Andes Press Agency;
p. 64: Hutchison Library; p. 65: David Richardson;
p. 67: Rex Features; p. 68: Andes Press Agency;
p. 70: Rex Features; p. 71: Andes Press Agency;
p. 72: Andes Press Agency; p. 73: Rex Features;
Camera Press; Free Federal Church Council.

Typographical design and typesetting by
VAP Publishing Services, Kidlington, Oxon.
Illustrations by Clyde Pearson
Printed by Bell and Bain Ltd, Glasgow

WEAVING TOGETHER

In each of these modules four strands of human experience will be woven together.

Family Community

Your experience is very important. You belong to a particular family group and you live in a particular place. You have your own interests and dreams.

Local Community

This strand looks beyond into the neighbourhood and the local community.

Plural Community

In this country there live followers of different religions. There are people who may have different family and religious customs from yours – your family customs may be different from the person sitting next to you. This makes life very interesting.

Global Community

In this strand you will learn how every country depends on other countries in all sorts of ways. You will reflect on how other parts of the world celebrate what is important in life: how communication is carried out and some of the difficulties there are and the values which are important.

Each module has tasks for you to do. Part of the work you will do, and it is a very important part, is the self-assessment tasks. These tasks are part of your learning. They will also give you a feed-back – that means that you will know how you are doing as you work through the module.

Religious education can be fun!

Communication   Celebration

Values

Let's get weaving

This module of work in your R.E. programme is called

Communication Level Two

It is all about analysing the importance of communication. You will examine different ways of communicating by reflecting on their effectiveness (whether they work well or not). You will also examine worship and prayer as ways in which religious people communicate with God.

Here are some of the things you will be doing in this module:

- **Exploring** communication as a way of keeping in touch.
- **Analysing** why people keep in touch.
- **Reflecting** on what makes communication effective.
- **Describing** times and places which are "special" for you.
- **Examining** the special times and places in religious worship including the Jewish synagogue.
- **Looking** at a special time for a Christian community in another part of the world.
- **Exploring** prayer as communication.
- **Reviewing** and assessing your learning.

RECALL

If you completed Communication Level 1 **Explain** the difference between verbal and non-verbal communication.

Draw what you consider to be an effective symbol.

Draw three important symbols used in Christianity.

1

Communication: keeping in touch

Communication can be about people keeping in touch with each other.

Task 1

Think about the different ways families keep in touch with each other.

Then explore how the local community organises its "communications".

KEEPING IN TOUCH

WHO? pen-pal family Australian aunt	HOW?	WHY?	Draw objects which make communication possible
Family Group Friends			
Local Community	Local Newspaper? Local Radio?		

Touch is an important way of communicating.

Young babies need to be held and handled. Touch can communicate love and care to a baby.

Would there be any point in telling a baby that you loved him/her? Discuss.

Can you think of any type or form of communication which is not shown above in the chart you have just completed?

Look at the illustrations below which may help you.

Choose one of them and write about a time when you used that particular form of communication.

Extension work

A
Use your imagination and *write* or *tell a story* about a rescue which was successful because of good communications.

B
Invent and *draw* a new form of communication which would make life easier for someone who is housebound.

2

Effective communication

Communication which gives the correct message

Task 2

Examine these examples of non-verbal communication and decide which signs are most effective – that is which signs give clear messages.

Write down what the message is.

Design a sign which is effective – which shows clearly what you mean – and then, try out your sign on the rest of your group or class.

Extension work

A

The above task examined visual communication.

Use the signs below to write your name. If others do not understand what each flag represents, then you will have written your name in code. What would be the *disadvantage* of using code?

B

Use the flag code to write welcome outside your classroom.

Find out who uses this flag code regularly and then *state* the advantages of using this as a form of communication.

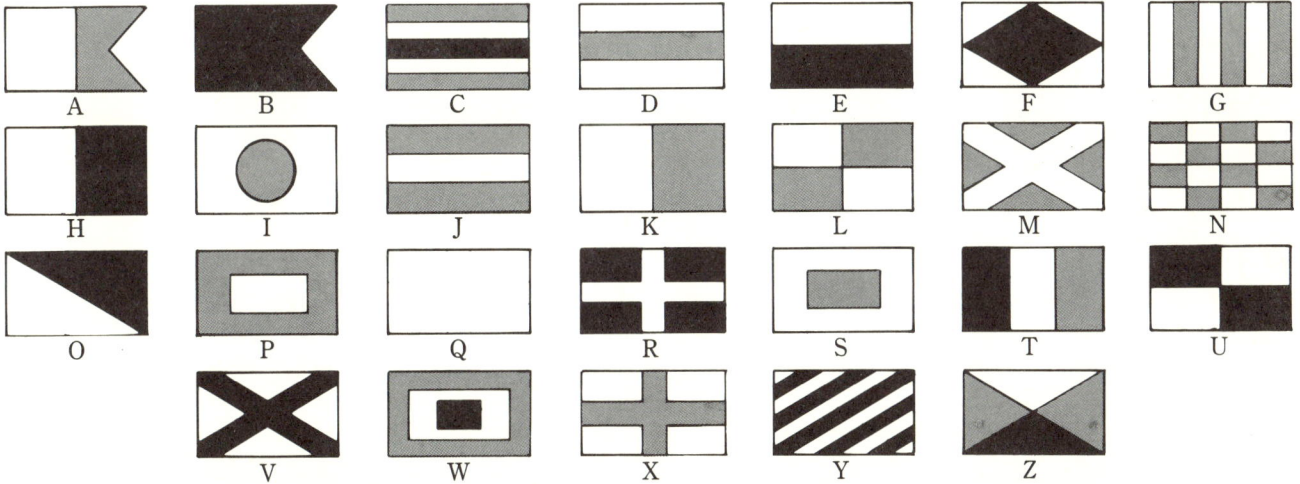

A	B	C	D	E	F	G

H	I	J	K	L	M	N

O	P	Q	R	S	T	U

V	W	X	Y	Z

Task 3

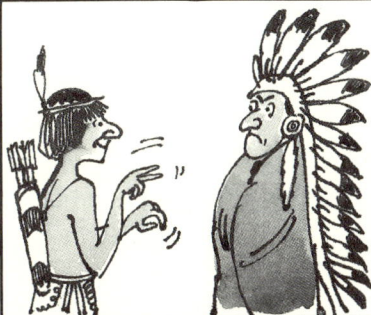

Language is one of the ways in which human beings communicate with one another. Language is not just words – there is also sign language which enables those who are deaf or unable to speak to communicate with other people.

Reflection

Reflection

What kind of language do you use?

Some people can be very clever with words. Write out or tell a joke to your partner. Jokes are ways of communicating funny events.

How do you react if someone praises you for something you have done?

How do you react if you know that someone is angry with you and uses angry words?

How do you react if someone has made you angry – do *you* use angry words?

You may have heard the expression. "It isn't what you say, but the way that you say it". What does this mean?

Extension work

A

Some homework! *Watch* the TV news one evening this week. *Make a note* of any news item which is about conflict. What kind of language is used to describe the situation?

B

Again, some work to do at home!

Listen to the kind of language which is used in advertisements for beauty treatment. How would you *describe* the language used by the advertisers? Is it persuasive? Why?

Task 4

Analyse what is happening in the cartoon.

What does the cartoon say about the ways in which we communicate with one another?

Does the cartoon say anything about the problems of communication?

Extension work

A

Has this ever happened to you? *Tell* your partner about it.

B

Write a five-minute speech about communication problems which someone your age might have. *Give* your speech to the rest of the class.

ASSESS your work!

Tasks 1–4

1. *Why do people keep in touch?*

   Name three ways of keeping in touch with someone who lives in another part of the world.

2. *What is effective communication?*

   Give one example of this.

3. *What kind of things hinder good communication?*

   Give some examples from your own experience.

Extension work

Did you attempt any of the extension work?

In the first three tasks you explored reasons for keeping in touch with other people. You also examined some non-verbal communication (flags and codes), as well as words as ways of communicating feelings and thoughts.

Places can also communicate

Task 5

Any place can become a "special place" because of the memories connected with it.

Read the following:

" Lynn, who is almost thirteen, had been coming to this place for over two years. No one knew about it except her. It was a quiet spot at the bottom of the garden which was so overgrown that it was used as the garden rubbish dump. Well that's what it looked like to anyone else but to Lynn it was a refuge. She liked thinking about it as a refuge, a place that was hers, where she could be quiet and calm, a special place. Over the years she had built up a sort of den. It was really no more than a shelter, but it was hers. Sometimes in the summer evenings she would sit in the old chair she had rescued from the dump and gaze out over the fields across the road. Lynn often thought that she was a strange mixture of a person. She loved being with her friends, managed to get on with her sisters and brother . . . most of the time . . . and yet she needed this private, special place. 'It's good to have time to myself, to think things over.' Lynn thought. Here, Lynn wrote her diary. She sometimes recorded not just what had happened to her, but also the changing views from her refuge with every passing season. She recorded the smells of spring and summer as well as early autumn. When winter came, she just came for a quick look, and then went inside for the warmth. "

Knowledge
Write what you know about Lynn's refuge.

Explain what a refuge is.

How would the view change with the changing seasons?

Understanding
Why did Lynn need a special place?

Extension work

A

What do you think about having a special place that is just yours?

Have you ever had a special place or refuge or den? If so *write* a description of it.

If you could create a refuge or a den what would it be like?

Write a poem entitled "My place . . ."

B

What makes special places "special"?

Do you have a special place for reading/thinking/praying . . .?

Draw or *paint* your special place.

Lynn's special place was a place where she could think. It was peaceful and calm there – Lynn's place gave her personal space!

Task 6 — Special times . . .

Just as there are places which are special to individuals, there are also times which are "special" times.

Read and reflect on what is written below.

Personal

I enjoy the time when the children are in bed asleep. I pick up the toys, tidy up a bit and then make myself a hot chocolate, with my feet up, my favourite magazine and some music on ..... this is the time when I feel I ....

Personal

Just before sunrise before the village is awake, I dress, slip out of the house and walk to the end of the village. Here I have a clear view of the mountains when the sun rises over the mountains I feel as if it's a brand new world and I'm brand new as well.

PERSONAL

AFTER SCHOOL, AFTER THE JOURNEY HOME ON THE NOISY SCHOOL BUS I GET HOME, GRAB A GLASS OF MILK AND A DIGESTIVE AND GO TO MY ROOM. I LIE ON MY BED, STARE AT THE CEILING. THIS IS THE BEST PART OF THE DAY FOR ME.

Extension work

A

Now *write* your own personal account of which times are special for you. And, say *why* . . .

B GROUP PROJECT

Choose one community of faith or worshippers. Make a *survey* of which times are "special" or sacred for them. Say *why*.

Going somewhere special?

Think about the last time you went somewhere special . . . now describe how you dressed?

Task 7

Write a short amusing story about someone who turns up for a school's country ramble, but is not properly or appropriately dressed.

When most people are invited to a special event or a special place, they take care to dress appropriately. This is a sign that you are happy to be a guest or to have been invited.

In this module you have already reflected on places and times which are special. Now think about the way people dress to express their thanks or their appreciation.

Extension work

A

Recall a time when you had to dress specially for an occasion.

B

Do some research. *What kind* of ceremonial dress is worn for the opening of parliament, and *why* is special dress worn?

What is being communicated by the special dress or clothing?

In worship, which is a way in which religious people communicate with God, there are special words, times, places and dress.

The Language of Worship

Special places

Worship is a form of communication for people who belong to particular faiths or religions.

AMEN } *Words*

HALLELUIA

HOSANNA

In an earlier task, you read that communication was about keeping in touch. Religious people believe that worship is a way of keeping in touch with God, and it is one of the ways in which God keeps in touch with human beings.

Special clothes

Movements

Think about these words, movements, special clothes and places. How might they help people to take part in worship?

Worship is a form of communication

Task 8

These signs and symbols are "international", that is, they are used in most parts of the world to communicate what they signify, what they point to.

Name each symbol/sign.
Discuss the importance of a common international "sign language".

These signs are self-explanatory because the number of meanings is restricted.

* These signs were used at the 1988 Olympic Games in Korea.

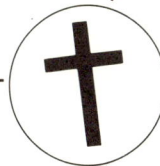

In Christian worship there is an "international language of communication" through symbolic objects, actions and gestures. Let's explore them.

Extension work

A and B Role-play

Devise a situation where you have problems in communication because you are in a foreign land.

Create a short five-minute sketch which involves four characters.

or

Explore the following situation in role-play: Jayne is "not talking" to her parents/or mother/ or father/or boyfriend.

The person who is being ignored by Jayne is desperately trying to resume communication. *Set up* the drama.

Task 9

Special occasions require special dress.

In many religions the person who leads the followers or believers often wears special clothes for this purpose. The special clothes are a sign that what is happening – public worship – is a special event.

The clothes may be traditional, by this is meant that the style of dress or robes has been handed down from a time in the past.

Let's look at the clothes that a Roman Catholic priest wears when he celebrates the Eucharist.

The special clothes or robes are called Vestments.

CHASUBLE   ALB   STOLE
When did priests begin
to dress like this?

Vestment: Garment, esp. official or state robe; any of the official garments of clergy, choristers, etc., worn during divine service.

Not all leaders of worship or religious services dress in this way.

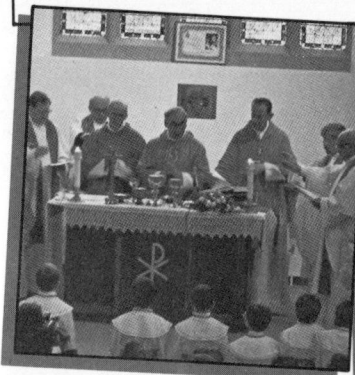

Extension work

A

Invite a local priest into class and ask him to *explain* why vestments have the names they have.

B

Find out why different colours are used for the priest's vestments at different times of the year.

Why are special clothes necessary?

Do Christian communities in other parts of the world have the same vestments or do they use clothes which belong to those particular countries?

Worship and special places

Earlier in this module you read that Worship is about communication. Special words and places and times and clothes are part of public worship.

Now you will explore some of the special objects which are used in public worship.

Public Worship

Public worship takes place in public places which may be specially set aside for this purpose.

Give some examples of special local buildings set aside for public worship.

Include examples of the variety of religions present in your local community.

Draw two of these and take care to represent the buildings as carefully as you can, taking into account the shape of the buildings and the name.

Make a copy of any notices which refer to the activities which take place in the particular buildings you are studying.

You may notice that some of the buildings are ordinary houses which are used for worship, and that some have a particular design.

Extension work

A

Visit a Christian place of worship and see how many of the objects shown below are to be seen. The purpose of your visit is to look at the variety of signs, symbols and objects used for worship or which are part of the surroundings of worship.

Often, these signs, symbols and objects communicate to the people involved, some of the meaning of worship.

These are some of the objects which may be seen in a Roman Catholic Church.

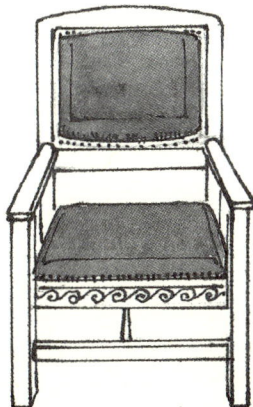

B

Reflect on the things you have at home which are only used for "special occasions" – or they might be too precious to use at all. These objects may be "special" because they were given by someone special to your family or because you brought a gift or made something when you were quite young. *Name* some of these and then *analyse* (say why) these objects are so special.

More about special places of worship

Worship reflects what the community believes about God

Task 11

Read the following:

Many Jews live in their traditional homeland – Israel, but most Jews do not live there. There are special historical reasons for this. Perhaps you can find out some of them.

Many hundreds of years ago, the main focus or centre of worship for the Jewish people was the Temple. In 587 BC the city of Jerusalem was destroyed and the people were taken off as captives or prisoners to Babylon.

As a way of keeping their faith alive, they met regularly for worship, sometimes outside and sometimes in buildings for the purpose of praying together. These buildings were like meeting houses and they were called Synagogues.

This is what the synagogue looks like from the gallery.

An aerial view.

The Greek word for a gathering together of people is
συναγογή
= synagogue.

Extension work

A

Michael is thirteen and is Jewish. He does not attend a Jewish school, he attends the local comprehensive school.

"I've tried to draw what my synagogue looks like. I hope you can make out what the synagogue looks like from my artistic impression!" Now *you* draw them!

B Research

Find out what the *Bimah, Ark* and *Menorah* are.

What is the *significance* of each?

What is happening here?

More about worship in the Synagogue

Task 12

Read the following:

While Jews can pray wherever they wish, there are three times a day when there should be prayer in the synagogue and in the home.

Morning Service

This service includes blessings, prayers, time for private prayer and readings from the Bible as well as readings from other books.

Kaddish is said or recited at each of the three daily services. Kaddish is an Aramaic word which means "sanctification". The prayer begins:

"Magnified and sanctified be His great Name in the world which He hath created according to His will. May He establish His Kingdom during His life, and during your days . . . speedily and at a near time."

Sons who say this prayer when their fathers have died, show them respect. When Kaddish is said or recited by mourners, those who are saddened by the death of friends or relatives, the congregation answers, "Let His great Name be blessed forever and to all eternity".

Extension work

A Jewish Prayer at home.

Examine the account of Jewish prayer below.

Prayer is a way of communicating with God and of God communicating with the person who is praying. In Jewish life and worship, prayer takes place at home as well as in the synagogue. Here is an example of the prayer which many Jewish families say at night.

> **PRAYERS BEFORE RETIRING TO REST AT NIGHT**
> Blessed art thou, O Lord our God, King of the universe, who makest the bands of sleep to fall upon mine eyes, and slumber upon mine eyelids. May it be thy will, O Lord my God and God of my fathers, to suffer me to lie down in peace and to let me rise up again in peace. Let not my thoughts trouble me, nor evil dreams, nor evil fancies, but let my rest be perfect before thee. O lighten mine eyes, lest I sleep the sleep of death, for it is thou who givest light to the apple of the eye. Blessed art thou, O Lord, who givest light to the whole world in thy glory.
> Taken from *Forms of Worship*

Write this prayer in your own words. Then underline the words which are not "everyday words".

Answer the following questions. How often are there services in the synagogue? Find out the times for these services. Perhaps you can contact the local synagogue and invite a member of the congregation to come along and talk to you.

What does Kaddish mean? Why do those who mourn pray for their dead? What does this say about their beliefs?

B

Another way of describing prayer is as a meeting with God.

Read the prayers on this page again.

What image of God is presented in them?

Why is the end of the day a "special" time for prayer?

Some Jews pray three times a day. What is the *significance* of "three" times? Can you think of any problems which might occur for someone who wishes to pray three times a day?

ASSESS your work!

Tasks 5–12

In Tasks 5–12 you thought about special places, times, clothes and objects which are used in worship.

1. *What would make a place special for you?*
2. *Why are special places used for worship?*
3. *Name the special place for worship which is used by members of the Jewish faith.*
4. *What is the difference between public and private worship?*
5. *What do you remember about any of the special religious objects you studied?*
6. *Draw two of them and write a few lines about their use.*

Before you move on . . .

● Look back over the tasks you have done.
● Have you any work to finish off?

Christian worship: special movements

"In worship it is important that body as well as mind is involved."

Task 13

Look at the gesture or symbolic postures which are shown below.

In groups of two or three, talk about what these postures suggest.

Many of these have become RITUALISED in Christian worship.

Extension work

A

Places of worship are symbolic of meeting-places or encounters with the God who is worshipped there.

Look at the design of several Christian churches. Why steeples? Why arch-shaped windows? Why an altar table? Why candles?

B

Ritual actions are symbolic of the attitudes which the believer has in the presence of God. Why use ritualised movements, like those above?

Kneeling   Standing   Joining hands

Shaking hands in peace   Gathering together

Hands raised in blessing   Gestures of sorrow and welcome

Role-play a story or message which uses some of these gestures. Try to communicate the message without words.

Task 14 — **"How are you feeling?"**

This is a reflection task which invites you to remember particular times or events in your life where the memories are quite strong.

1. Recall a time when you were amazed at something marvellous.
2. Recall a time when you wondered what life was all about.
3. Recall a time when you felt really glad to be alive.
4. Recall a time when you felt in danger.
5. Recall a time when you knew that other people really loved you.
6. Recall a time when you were sorry about something you had done.
7. Recall a time when you asked someone to forgive you.
8. Recall a time when you felt like thanking someone very much.

If you want to, you can share some of these experiences with your partner, or in a group.

For many people some of the experiences which are mentioned above are religious experiences – they are times when a person knows that God is present in the experience. A person may look at a sunset or a new baby and praise and thank God in her/his heart.

Prayer is a conversation with God

All good conversations need times for listening as well as times for talking.

Extension work

A and **B**

If you pray, you may want to fill in the following. Copy the chart into your file or workbook. Do not write in this book.

I usually pray when ....

Sometimes when I pray I...

A prayer I often say is...

....taught me to pray.

....prayer is like ....

In school prayer is ....

Prayer and worship in the community

Task 15

Read the following:

A community is a group that shares common interests. A community of believers share the same beliefs about God. These communities come together at special times and on special days. These communities come together to worship as a community.

If you belong to a group, the group can help you when you are in trouble or worried.

Religious communities or communities of faith (communities which share the same beliefs in God) find help and strength when they come together.

The members of the community who are not present at the public worship are also remembered. During the religious service, there may be a time when those who are absent are remembered – they are also part of the community.

At a Sunday celebration of Mass, the Eucharist, some members who are at the service, will take Communion to those members of the community or Parish who are not able to attend. This special role in the community is called "Eucharistic minister".

Extension work

A

Find ten people who attend community worship regularly. Ask them why they do so.

Make a note of their responses and present them to the rest of the class.

B

Why is it important to remember those members of the community who are not able to attend community worship?

How do TV religious programmes involve viewers in worship?

Worship and celebration

In worship Christians believe that they communicate with God. Their belief in God gives sense and meaning to human life. So when they worship Christians also celebrate the gift and purpose of life. Like other religious communities, Christians celebrate important occasions in the life of a person.

Here are some of them.

Birth Growth Marriage Death

For many people, these are the times when they take part in public worship.

Extension work

A

What is there to celebrate?

Interview a couple who have celebrated a wedding anniversary.

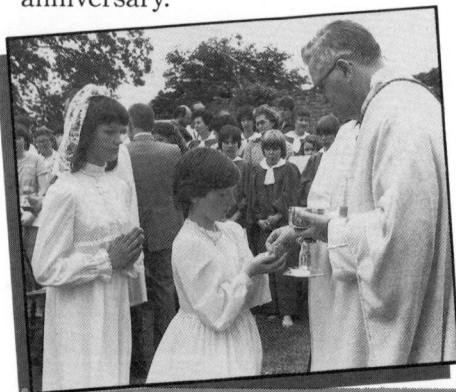

B

Roman Catholic children make a celebration of "First Communion". *Find out* what happens and why it is a celebration.

or

Choose a celebration which takes place in Judaism, *find out* why the celebration takes place in the synagogue: for example, *Bar Mitzvah*.

Task 16   Research

Look at your local newspaper. Turn to the page where there are announcements about births/engagements/wedding anniversaries.

Make a list of the kind of events which people celebrate. Now compare this with the local newsletter from a Church or religious community.

Mr and Mrs Brown celebrated their Golden Wedding Anniversary yesterday. Before the family (including 5 sons and daughters, 8 grandchildren and 2 great-grandchildren) met at a local hotel for a celebration meal, the family returned to the Church of St Paul, where the couple were married 50 years ago . . .

Worship – the global strand

Have you ever been to a Harvest Festival or seen or heard about this celebration?

If you have, tell the rest of your class what happens.

Harvest Festivals are religious events. The community thanks God for all that has grown in the fields during the Spring and the Autumn.

Why have a celebration of Harvest?

Does the Harvest mean anything to people who live in towns and cities?

A young boy brought up in the city once expressed surprise to discover that milk came from cows. "We get ours from bottles, Miss".

Read the account below of the Celebration of the Harvest and Levy (Tax) in a town in Northern Nigeria. It was written by Adem Emaiku.

Hello, my name is Adem and I'm 13 years old. My mother is english and my father is nigerian: they met each other when they were students. My dad came to London to study. Every two years I get the chance to visit my grandparents in Ilorin — about 3½ hours drive from the capital — Lagos. My last visit was great! I love the sun and meeting all my relations. (I also had three weeks off school to make the visit worthwhile!)

While I was there, our Parish in Ilorin was celebrating Harvest. The church was decorated with palms and leaves and all the people wore their best clothes. Every person in the Parish danced (yes danced!) up with some fruits of the harvest. There was so much to give thanks for. Every woman who had had a baby since the last Harvest, danced with the baby on her back, in procession. Every father — every young person; all farmers and carpenters... "Anyone who has thanks to give to God — come dance in worship."

I danced too! It is good to be with my father's people. Every person in the Parish also donates some money — called a Levy — for the Parish funds.

Adem.

1. What was Adem doing in Nigeria?
2. What celebration did he take part in?
3. What is a Harvest celebration? Have you ever taken part in a Harvest celebration?
4. If you had to describe Adem's Harvest celebration, what words would you use?
5. How would you feel if dance were part of worship in this country?

Extension work

A

Find out what happens in a local Church when it is Harvest time?

Draw some of the fruits of Harvest in this country.

What types of fruit would be harvested in Nigeria?

B

What is the *relationship* between Harvest festivals and "giving thanks"?

What does dance *express* or *communicate* in worship?

AH!
qu'il
EST BON
LE
BON
DIEU

The motto of the Sisters of Notre Dame. What does the motto mean?

Extension work

A

Find out if there are any religious communities of priests, brothers or sisters near your school. Arrange a *visit* or *invite* a speaker.

CASE STUDY:

Worship in a religious community.

There are many different ways of being a Christian in today's world. Some women feel called by God to live out Christianity in a way where everything which they have and own is shared with members of the community. The work which they do is also shared. Below is an account of a community of religious sisters who live and work in Liverpool.

"Our community house, or convent is part of a large college campus. There are just under 2,000 students, of all ages here. Most of them live at home but about 600 live in student accommodation.

Every morning and evening the community meets to pray together, and those students who are interested join us. We say what is called the "prayer of the Church" – all priests, brothers, nuns and sisters use this. The morning prayer thanks and praises God for the new day. The evening prayer thanks God for all that the day has brought. In morning and evening prayer, the community remembers the poor, the sick and all those in special need.

Not all the sisters work with students – some do social work in Liverpool and one is a student. There are some retired sisters who always meet whoever calls at the community house with a warm welcome and a cup of coffee.

The prayer, the welcomes and the work are all part of the community's way of living the Christian gospel.

Often the sisters have many visitors from other parts of the world who are also members of their religious community.

B

Just as there are Christians all over the world, there are also religious communities all over the world. *Find out* about a religious community whose main work is in another part of the world.

ASSESS your work!

Tasks **13–18**

1. *Prayer and worship involves the body as well as the mind.*

   What special movements are sometimes used in worship?

2. *Did you explore your feelings in Task 14?*

   Did you discover anything about yourself?

3. *Name three important celebrations in the lifetime of a person.*

   Did you complete any of the Extension work?

   Before you move on to the next tasks, look back over your work and see if there is any work which is incomplete.

Let's explore varieties of Christian prayer

In every religion, prayer or meditation is a way of worshipping, keeping in touch with God.

Earlier in this module you read that prayer could be like having a conversation with God, and all good conversations need times for listening as well as times for speaking.

Extension work

A and B

What is your *experience* of any of the kinds of prayer mentioned above? If you want to, you can *share* your experience with others.

Task 19

Look at the variety or kinds of prayer below.

Match each description to a word that describes it.

You may want to do this with the other members of your class group, or quietly by yourself.

- An old man sat in Church for hours, day after day. "What are you doing?" "I look at God and God looks at me."
- "Speak Lord your servant is listening."
- "For mountain bikes, school holidays and good health. Thanks."
- It's the Lord!
- God grant me patience.
- Praise God in the heavens and on the earth . . .

- ASKING   • RECOGNIZING   • THANKING
- PRAISING   • LISTENING   • BEING WITH

Task 20

Read the prayers below which are used in public worship by most Christian traditions and then answer the questions.

66 Holy, holy, holy, Lord, God of power and might, 99

This is a prayer of praise. *What is praise? Have you ever praised anyone?*

66 Lamb of God, you take away the sins of the world: have mercy on us. Lamb of God, you take away the sins of the world: have mercy on us. Lamb of God, you take away the sins of the world: grant us peace. 99

66 Glory be to the Father and the Son and to the Holy Spirit, Amen. 99

This prayer asks for forgiveness. *What is mercy? Why would humans ask God for mercy? Can humans be merciful?*

In this prayer God is Father, Son and Spirit – the Trinity. What does this mean to you?

Extension work

A

Write your own poem or song of praise. *Illustrate* your work and display it in your classroom.

B

Re-read the prayer that begins, "Lamb of God . . ."

Which areas of our world are in need of peace? At home? Locally? Globally?

Let's explore some of the prayers from Christian tradition

Task 21

Read the following:

66 Three things O Lord I pray:
to know thee more clearly,
love thee more dearly,
follow thee more nearly. 99

(St. Richard's prayer)†

66 Hail Mary, full of grace, the Lord is with thee,*
blessed art thou among women and blessed is the fruit
of thy womb Jesus.
Holy Mary Mother of God
pray for us sinners now and
at the hour of our death. Amen. 99

66 Make me a channel of your peace
where there is despair, let me bring hope.
Where there is hurt, let me bring pardon,
where there is fear, let me bring love.
O Master, help me to serve others rather than expect
to be served by them . . .
for it is when we give
that we receive
and in dying that we are born into
eternal life. 99

(prayer attributed to St. Francis)†

66 Christ be near at either hand,
Christ above, below me stand
Christ with me wherever I go 99
Christ above, behind, below.

(St. Patrick's breastplate)†

** Find the place near the beginning of Luke's gospel, where
these words are written.*

*† Choose one of these saints: who was he?
Do some research.*

Extension work

A

Many traditional prayers are
often illustrated or written in
special ways.

Choose one of these traditional
prayers and *illustrate* it.

B

Research your own tradition or
a tradition which you have an
interest in for other prayers
which are often used.

or

Ask parents, teachers/class for
their favourite prayers and
compile an *anthology*.

More about movement and prayer

Task 22

Read the following:

Earlier in this module you reflected on the fact that human beings have bodies as well as spirits. When people worship, they use their bodies to show what they believe about God.

Many religions use "joined hands" to show the importance of prayer.

This gesture shows that the important thing at that particular moment is to concentrate on God, to set aside all the activities that keep people and hands busy, and to make time for God.

Kneeling is a gesture which says that a person is in the presence of a God who is mighty and powerful: it can also symbolize a person's need for forgiveness.

Extension work

A GROUP WORK

Read the account of the Creation in the first chapter of the book of Genesis.

In your group, work out the kind of movements which express the different parts of the Creation account.

You may decide to use music. Ask your teacher what kind of music would help create the right atmosphere.

You may decide to rewrite the account in your own words. Why not perform your dance for a class assembly?

B

Choose a Christian hymn and express it in dance and movement.

Prayer and worship are ways of communicating with God and ways in which God communicates with human beings. People who believe in God believe that God "speaks" to them through the events of their lives as well as through the special times of prayer and worship. Some people say that all of life is about worshipping God. Look at the cartoons below. Do you think these people could be worshipping God? How?

Task 23

People who pray believe that they are in touch with God. They believe that praying is one of the ways of keeping in touch with God. Prayer whether in public or private is a way of worshipping and COMMUNICATING with God.

Extension work

A and B

Draw your own picture to illustrate or show the same message as the pictures above.

Read the following account about a man of prayer.

Thomas Merton

When Tom was a young man he really enjoyed life. He had lots of girl friends and parties to go to. He went to university in England and as an American abroad he enjoyed university life to the full. His life was full of interesting places to go and things to do. He was not a very religious young man – quite the opposite in fact.

Tom enjoyed the company of friends he had at university. He had been brought up by his grandparents. When his grandfather died, Tom was very upset and very sad. That night Tom did something which was very unusual for him. He knelt by the side of his bed and he prayed. During the next week he visited churches and was present at a Roman Catholic Mass. He did not know what was going on, but he felt somehow attracted to this way of worshipping. Later he went back to the church to pray. When he was 23 he decided to become a Roman Catholic. Later he visited a monastery which was the home of some Trappist monks. Trappists live a very hard life with little sleep, little conversation and no meat. Their whole life from the time they get up in the early hours of the day (you might call it the middle of the night) to the short time when sleep is allowed, every action and thought and word is directed towards God.

In this strange place, Tom found the peace he was searching for. He stayed. Soon he was a monk. He continued to write books. Although he was in a monastery he became very involved in what was happening in the outside world. The monks' prayers and life apart from the everyday lives of most people did not mean that they were not concerned with life.

Tom wrote about the need for peace and the need for governments to stop making plans for war. He became very famous. His life as a monk and a man of prayer involved him deeply in the concerns of the world.

Now answer these questions

Knowledge

1. Write a short account of what Tom's life was like before he became a man of prayer.
2. What event changed the whole direction of Tom's life?
3. What did Tom do then?
4. Was this a strange thing to do?

Extension work

A Understanding

1. Why would an event like the death of someone close cause Tom to think about his life?
2. Did anything in Tom's life before he became a monk show that he might be drawn to the life of a monk?
3. Why do monks live apart from others?
   If you do not know, then find out!
4. Why would Tom be searching for peace?

B Evaluation

What do you think about Tom's decision to become a monk?

Is it usual for monks who have "left" society to become famous men when they have left the ordinary world behind?

What is the purpose of the kind of life that monks live?

What do you think about the monk's way of life?

As well as Christian monks there are also Buddhist monks in Britain.

Find out what you can about any community of monks.

Task 25

Read the following:

John Smith also prays. He isn't a monk – he's seventeen and works on a YTS scheme. Religion is a very important part of his life. As well as spending half an hour at the beginning of each day, he is a member of a prayer group which meets every Thursday evening. He says, "prayer keeps me in touch with myself and with God . . . I need it like I need fresh air to breathe . . ."

Is prayer important for John?
How do you know?

What does "prayer keeps me in touch with myself" mean?
And what does "I need it like I need fresh air to breathe", mean?

Jesus teaches people to pray

Read how Christians find Jesus' teaching about prayer helpful.

For Christians, the words that Jesus said and the actions or things he did are very important.

In the Gospels, there are many times when Jesus prays, and on one occasion, the disciples who were his special followers asked him to teach them to pray.

RECALL

Jesus taught them what is called the Lord's prayer or the Our Father. See Level 1, Task 23.

Task 26

Choose one of the stories below which will tell you something about what Jesus taught about prayer.

Write what was said in your own words and then write what you think about it.

| Matthew 6:5–15 | Matthew 7:7–13 |

What do these stories say about the kind of God that God is?

Extension work

A

Find another example of anything Jesus said about prayer. *Write* what it *means* in your own words.

B

There is a custom in Buddhism that prayers are written down on papers. The papers are then attached to trees outside the Buddhist Temple. The belief is that the concerns, the prayers written on the papers, will find favour with the good spirits.

What do you think of this way of praying? If you had to write your own concerns or the concerns your school has on these "prayer papers", what would you write?

21

Tasks 19–26

Recall the different types of prayer. (Task 19).

Can you remember any traditional Christian prayer? Write it down.

How does movement help some people to pray?

Did you do any research into monks and monasteries? What did you discover?

Why do people pray?

Did you do any extension work?

Review of the module

- Look over the work you have done in this module.
- Which work did you find most interesting?
- Which tasks would you like to improve?
- Have you any ideas for any Tasks which would make the module more interesting?
- Did you make any visits to any places of prayer?
- Would it have helped to see a monastery or a convent?
- Any other comments?

How did we do?

Managing your own learning

We are the Champions!

Were you

1. Usually on time for class/usually late for class?
2. Hardworking . . . most of the time/some of the time/not very often?
3. Able to work by yourself sometimes?
4. Able to work with others in a group?

Did you

5. Find the work very easy or very difficult?
6. Work when the teacher was busy with other people or only when the teacher was with you?
7. Cooperate with the teacher?
8. Did you follow up any of the work you did at home by reading or finding out more about any of the topics you have covered?
9. Did you do any extension/project work?

Do you

10. Find it easy to tell the teacher of any problems you had?
11. Prefer to work by yourself or with others?

Now, share what you have done with your class teacher.

Well done!

you have completed Communication, Level Two

This module of work in your R.E. programme is called

Celebration *Level Two*

It is all about how people celebrate the experience of being set free – especially in Judaism and Christianity.

Here are some of the things you will be doing in this module:

- **analysing** how people celebrate being free.
- **finding** out about slavery.
- **doing** a project on a group suffering a form of injustice.
- **reflecting** on what can be done to help such a group.

- **analysing** the passover-exodus experience.
- **examining** the celebration of Pesach by Jews today.
- **exploring** the Christian festival of Holy Week and Easter.
- **tracing** links between the celebration of the Eucharist and the central events of Christianity and Judaism.
- **reflecting** on Christianity as a commitment to the poor.

RECALL

If you completed Celebration Level One, **review your work on Celebration in the Level One Module.**

Do you *recall*:

- **describing** some celebration in your family and local community?
- **exploring** the Chinese New Year festival?
- **discovering** about the Sacred Thread ceremony in Hinduism?
  and Amrit in Sikhism?
  and Confirmation in Christianity?
- **exploring** festivals in Hinduism and Christianity?

Which part of the module did you feel you did best at the time?

What do the following words mean . . .

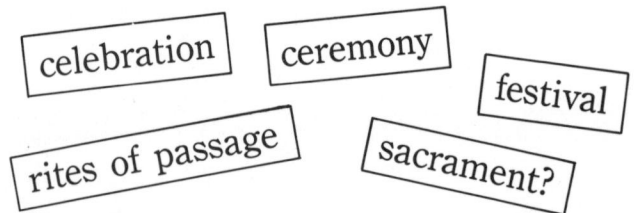

celebration   ceremony   festival

rites of passage   sacrament?

How much of the extension work did you do?

If you are new to this programme

WELCOME

Freedom

This module is about celebrating freedom, and in the first part of it you will be exploring your experience of freedom. Before you do that, read this short story. It's called

An unexpected freedom

Lynn and Ian usually looked forward to their weekend visits to their grandparents. However, it was with some reluctance that they bought their train tickets and set off for Colwyn Bay this weekend.

Until the School Football Team managed to get into the county finals, Ian had really wanted to help Grandad paint the garage as well as mend the felt on the garage roof. Now Colwyn Bay seemed an unattractive proposition. Usually he couldn't wait to get away from the city. He loved the freedom he had at his grandparents' house and he also loved being near the sea. But this weekend . . .

Lynn wasn't too happy about the visit because she knew that Ian would be miserable most of the time and that he would moan to her about missing the match, while pretending to be really happy to their grandparents.

Granny met them at the railway station. She seemed a bit worried.

"This is awful – you'll have to go straight back home. After you left your Aunt Nicole arrived from Paris, and as she's leaving first thing in the morning Mum and Dad think you ought to see her before she flies out. Grandpa is in the car and we'll all drive back to Liverpool."

Ian could hardly hide his delight – now, he could really look forward to the match.

Task 1

Can you think of times when you were given an unexpected freedom from doing something you did not particularly like and being able to do something more pleasing to you – for example, a day off school?

With your partner, think of as many examples as you can. For each example, fill in a table like this one.

Example of freedom given:	
Who gave you the freedom? Why did they do that?	
How did you feel when you found out you were free?	
Would you have liked to be free like that for ever? Say why or why not.	
What were you freed *from* doing?	
What were you free *to do*?	

Extension work

A

Make a list of *five* unexpected freedoms you wish you had now.

Are there any of these you are unlikely ever to have?

How do you feel about that?

B

Describe the times when you feel *most* free and *least* free to do things you would like to do.

Free from...

Many people experience a longing to be free from something which stops them living life freely and happily.

Look at these letters to the Agony Aunt in a magazine.

> Dear Jane,
> Some years ago I stole some money from work and someone else got the blame and was sacked. I was too frightened to own up at the time and now I just can't sleep at night thinking about the wrong I did – how can I ever be forgiven? John, Cardiff.

> Dear Aunt Jane
> My parents are driving me mad with their constant arguing and rowing. I'd give anything not to have to live in this atmosphere all the time.
> Sue, 14, Lincoln.

> Dear Jane
> I haven't told anyone at home about this, my dad would go daft, but I can't stop playing fruit machines. I spend everything I've got, and I've started stealing to get money to gamble. I've tried giving it up but I just keep going back.
> Steve, 13, Bristol.

> Dear Jane
> My mother is in her 70's and can't look after herself so she lives with us. She can't really be left on her own anymore, so it's four years since we had a holiday or even a night out. I don't know how much more I can take.....
> M.B. Leeds.

Task 2 GROUP WORK

After you have read the letters to Aunt Jane

Analyse: what it is the writers long to be free from

Discuss: what other kinds of things people in families and groups in your community long to be free from and

Make a list of them.

Here are some words which may help to get you started – but you may need to look some of them up in your dictionary.

grief

isolation   hypothermia   prejudice   conflict

Make a chart like this, and fill it in

People in . . .	Want to be free from . . .
families	
school	
our street	
our town or district	

Extension work

A

Ask some people, at home and in your neighbourhood, what things they would like to be free from.

Write a report on what you find out.

B

If you were Aunt Jane, *what advice* would you give to the people who have written in? *Discuss* with your partner and *compose* your answer as it would appear in the magazine.

26

Freedom to...

Sometimes people are not free to do what they have a right to do.

For example:

Everybody has a *right* to learn at school without being bullied by anybody in the school. So if your school is *free from* bullying, you are *free to* get on with learning in a safe place, a freedom which you have a *right* to. When people have legitimate RIGHTS, other people have a DUTY to respect those rights and not take them away.

Whose **rights** are being denied in these pictures. Are people free to do whatever they like?

Task 3

Think of one time or incident in your life when someone else's action stopped you doing what you wanted to do.

Discuss the incident with your partner and then listen to your partner's experience.

In your groups, Brainstorm *the rights that people of your age should have – wherever they live.*

Rank or group them in order of importance.

Decide whether you think these rights are generally respected in your community and elsewhere. Pool and collate (collect together) your ideas, and display them.

Rights	Respected	
	Here	Elsewhere
1		
2		
3		
4		
5		
6		
7		

Extension work

A

Role-play a situation where somebody of your age is denied a basic right.

B

What do people in that situation feel? What can they do?

Freedom: a global viewpoint

So far you have been thinking about people in your local community longing to be free from all the various things that get people down and stop them from living happy and peaceful lives. But, of course, there are whole regions of the world, and whole nations, where people long to be free.

Task 4

With your partner: make a list of the kind of things that whole regions or countries long to be free from; say what it is and which countries are involved.

*In your class group: pool your ideas and colour-code the kinds of things that people may feel **Oppressed** by or **Threatened** by.*

For example:

War – orange
Drought – purple
Lack of religious freedom – green
Epidemic – yellow **Anything else . . . ? –**

Poverty
Injustice – blue

Locate suitably coloured flags or stickers on an outline map or globe.

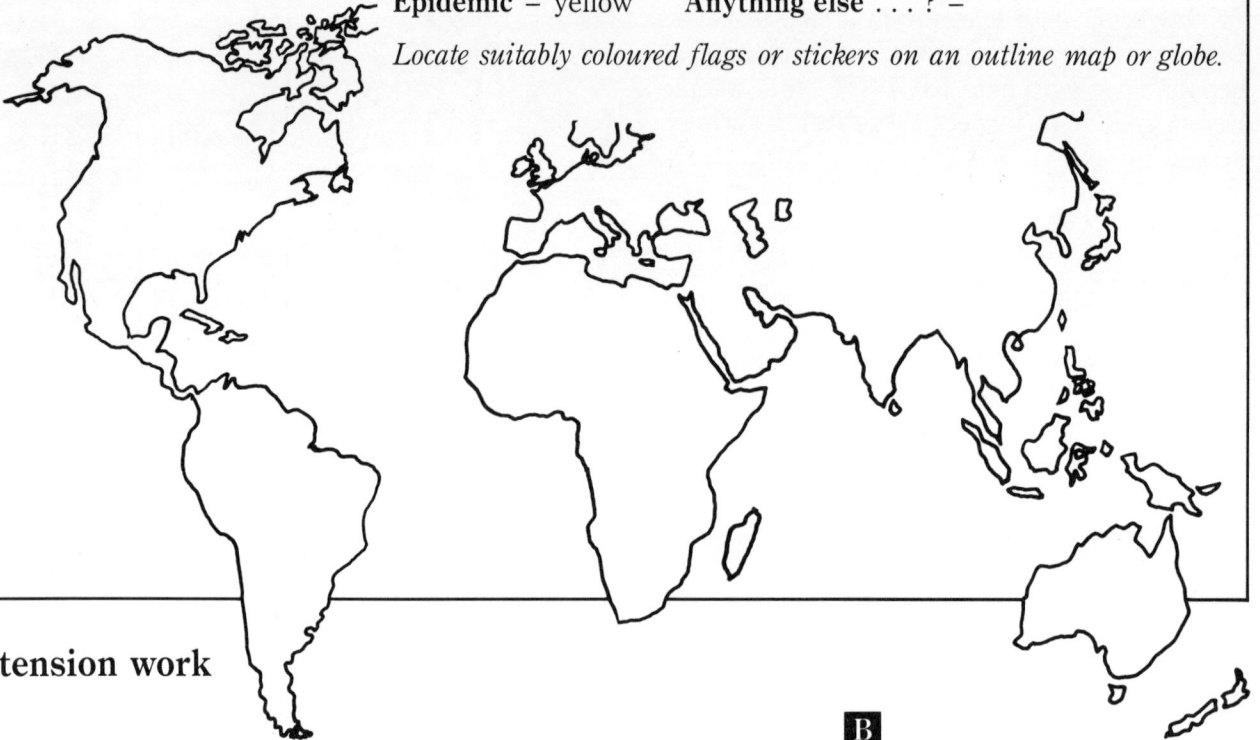

Extension work

A

Take ONE example of a region or nation longing to be free and *explain* what the basic problem is, as far as you can be sure from the information you have.

B

Identify how many of the situations have to do with religion.

Celebrating freedom

When people have been longing for freedom or involved in a long struggle for freedom and then become free to live their lives happily and peacefully, or with some hope about the future, they usually celebrate and continue to remember how they became free and the people who helped to bring it about.

The Batesons were having tea.

"Hey, Mum," said Colin, "this is a bit special for a Tuesday, isn't it?"

"Yes it is, but I thought I'd remind you of something special that happened to me, Colin."

"I know," said Kim, "it's a year ago today that you came home from hospital and we had that party."

They all went quiet, remembering the difficult months that had led up to that day.

Task 5

Read the story and then consider if you or anyone you know has had a similar experience. Tell your partner about it, or put the story on tape or in writing in your file.

It could be about the end of a long period of worry, or fear, or coming to the end of a long struggle over exams or a term's work. Anything that deserved a celebration in the end. How did you celebrate?

Find a way of displaying your work on this task.

"I won't forget the day you collapsed, love," said Ted Bateson. "When they rang me at work I got such a shock, and by the time I got to the hospital and saw you, it was obvious there was something seriously wrong."

"I must have looked like I felt, then!"

Shirley Bateson recalled the pain, and the panic, and the loneliness she felt as the ambulance dashed through the streets with lamps flashing and siren wailing.

"The last thing I remember of the journey was the ambulance lady holding my hand and whispering 'you'll be all right, you'll see'."

She had been on a life-support machine for a fortnight, and at one stage the doctors had told Colin that things did not look too good. He'd sat at her bedside day and night, whispering encouragement but feeling very afraid. Then one morning the fever had subsided and Shirley began the long, slow road to recovery.

"Weren't the nurses marvellous, Ted."

"I remember that bloke they all called Mr Sunshine," Colin said.

"Yes, he'd had the same thing and got better, and carried on visiting the ward for years after, cheering everybody up."

"But the day you came home was best – that really was something to celebrate," said Kim.

There was quiet again for a moment, then Colin reached for a cream cake . . .

Extension work

A

Find out about how a community you know about *celebrates* a special occasion when people became free.

For example:

> Remembrance Sunday
> Bastille Day
> or a local event.

Analyse the celebration:

- What did the community long to be free from?
- How did it achieve freedom?
- Who led the community in its search?
- How is the occasion remembered and celebrated?
- How is the memory of the freedom-fighters celebrated?
- Why do people carry on celebrating people and events of the past in the present?
- In what ways have people today benefited from the efforts of earlier communities to secure freedom?

B

Research the movements that led to the vote being given to women, or the passing of laws about child labour in Britain. Use the questions in part A of the extension work as a guide for your research.

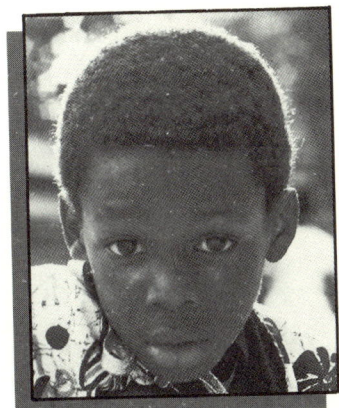

In Tasks 1–5 you have been exploring and analysing freedom and how people celebrate being free.

1. *In Task 1 you were invited to recall the experience of being given an unexpected freedom.*
   How many examples did you manage to think of?
   Which occasion gave you the most pleasure?
   Did you manage the extension work?

2. *Did you enjoy the work on the letters to Aunt Jane's agony column in Task 2?*
   How long a list did you make?
   Did you produce a report or compose some replies to the letters?

3. *What did you learn about freedom around the world?*
   Did your class group display a colour-coded map?
   In the extension work, what problem did you focus on, or what did you find out about the religious basis of some of these struggles?

4. *Which freedom is celebrated most in your community?*
   Did you manage to display your work?

5. *Has the work so far helped you to understand more about some of the issues involved in struggling for freedom and celebrating it when it is achieved?*

Review of the module

- Do you think you have made a good start to this module?
- What are you particularly proud of in the work you have done?
- What could you improve on in the rest of the module? Set yourself a target.

Slavery and the right to be a free person

What is it like to be owned by somebody else and treated as their property?

For more than 300 years traders from England, especially from ports like Plymouth and Liverpool, became rich by sailing the Slave Trade Triangle.

Investigating the Slave Trade

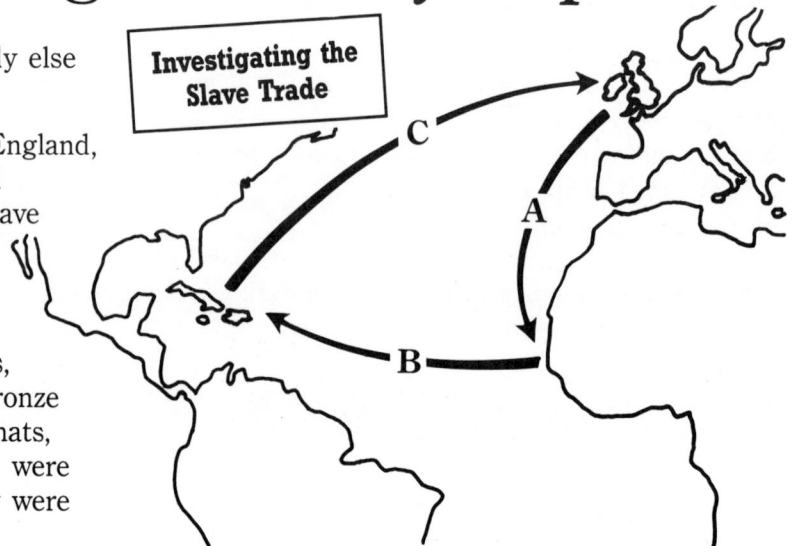

A Goods made in England – muskets, gunpowder, cutlery, copper rods, bronze rings (used as money), gunpowder, felt hats, glass, beads, spirits, tobacco and beer – were shipped to the African coast where they were exchanged for slaves.

B The journey from Africa to the Caribbean – the Middle Passage – was terrible because of the awful conditions on the ships, and many of the slaves died before reaching the West Indies. Many of the crew also became diseased and died.

C The slaves were sold to the owners of plantations in exchange for sugar, rum, molasses, spices and tobacco. The plantation owners wanted the slave labour so that they could produce the crops profitably and meet the increased demand for sugar for people in England, for example.

Slaves in England

Many of the wealthy planters and traders brought their own slaves back to England with them, and very soon it became common to see very young black slaves in the service of wealthy traders, ships' captains, government officials and military officers coming back from abroad, and the captains of merchant ships.

One of the first and wealthiest traders in slaves was Sir John Hawkins, who sailed from Plymouth, on one occasion with a ship and crew loaned to him by Queen Elizabeth I; with goods to exchange for slaves in West Africa. He then transported his slaves by sea to the New World, exchanging them for goods such as tobacco or for much larger sums of money than he had paid. On return to Plymouth, he sold the goods at great profit and soon became one of the richest people in England as did many traders who took a lead from him.

TO BE SOLD
BY PUBLIC AUCTION,
On MONDAY the 18th of MAY, 1829,
UNDER THE TREES,
FOR SALE,
THE THREE FOLLOWING
SLAVES
viz.
HANNIBAL, about 30 Years old, an excellent House Servant, of Good Character.
WILLIAM, about 35 Years old, a Labourer.
NANCY, an excellent House Servant and Nurse.
The MEN belonging to LEECES' Estate, and the WOMAN to Mrs D. SMIT

Also for Sale, at Eleven o'Clock,
Fine Rice, Gram, Paddy, Books, Muslin, Needles, Pins, Ribbons, &c, &c.

Slaves were sold to the highest bidders at auctions like the one advertised in this poster.

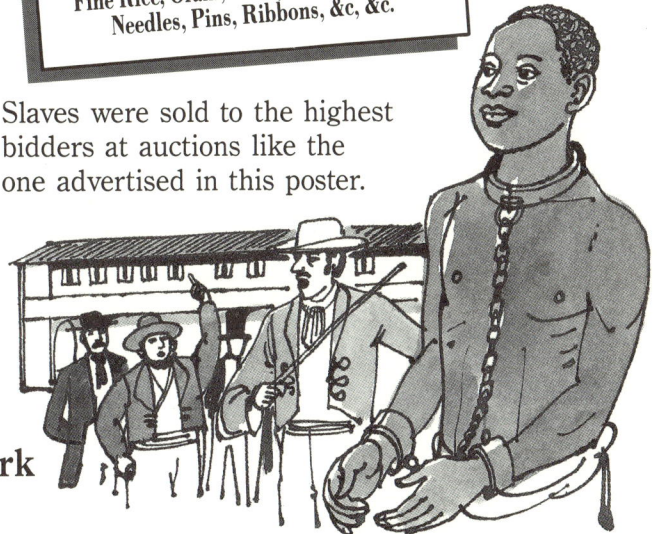

Task 6

Using the information here and in your school library or history text-books, analyse the role played by people involved in the growth of the slave trade.

- *Why were the slaves needed?*
- *Who profited from the slave trade?*
- *How did slaves come to be in England?*
- *Who would be most threatened by moves to abolish slavery?*

Extension work

A

Re-create imaginatively the story of a West African boy or girl taken as a slave to be sold and to work on plantations in the West Indies and America. *Tape-record* or *write down* your story.

B

Many of the slave-traders were Christians. Here is how they justified their trade.

"The people we take to plantations enjoy a better life than they would have had staying in Africa. They were not really human like us anyway, and their labour is needed to keep the plantations going. Even if we stopped slave-trading, other countries could take our place and our profits, they would still become slaves and people in Britain would lose their jobs and good income."

What do you think about these arguments?

The fight against slavery

In the last task you were analysing how the slave trade developed. The next part of the module deals with how slavery came to be abolished in Britain.

Task 7 *Analyse how slaves came to be liberated.*

You should examine the evidence about the fight against slavery and then see if you can tell your partner some of the reasons why slavery was eventually abolished.

Here are some points to consider:

1. Slaves in Britain and the colonies set themselves free.
   Many slaves ran away and were helped by other blacks and sympathetic whites. In Jamaica the runaways, called the Maroons, set up communities in the hills, and fought for their freedom. Black servants began to resist the authority of their owners, and so helped to free themselves.

2. Black people in Britain who had become free worked for the abolition of slavery. Olaudah Equiano wrote the story of his own move from slavery to freedom, and became a spokesman against slavery for the black community.
   He said there was plenty of profit to be made trading goods with Africa, without trading people.

3. The poorer and working-class people of the time in Britain supported the fight of the black community against slavery. In Manchester, in the 19th century, over 20,000 people signed a petition calling for abolition.

4. A religious group, the Quakers, who believe in peaceful ways of bringing about change, were very active in the fight against slavery in Britain and America.

5. In the end, the slave trade was seen as being not very profitable anymore.

Extension work

A

Hold a debate, *role-playing* the views of the Abolitionists and of those who were in favour of slave-trading.

B

William Wilberforce was a Member of Parliament for Hull and dedicated himself to bringing about new laws which would abolish the slave trade. Those who wanted slavery abolished were called Abolitionists – people like Granville Sharpe who was so moved by the sight of a slave who had been beaten up and left to die by his owner that he took him to hospital. The slave, Jonathan Strong, recovered and was recaptured by his owner who wanted to sell him off again into slavery in the West Indies. Sharpe heard about this and got Strong released, and spent many years trying to make sure that such a thing could not happen again in England. Eventually he persuaded the Lord Chief Justice to declare that buying and selling people in England was unlawful, but the slave trade still continued. In Parliament, William Wilberforce tried year after year to get slavery abolished, but without success. There were too many wealthy and powerful people who stood to lose millions of pounds if the trade in slaves was stopped. Wilberforce continued to gather information about the cruel way that slaves were treated, and the inhuman conditions that they suffered during their journeys west. It was more than forty years later, in 1833, and shortly after Wilberforce's death, that his supporters carried through Parliament the Bill for the Abolition of Slavery, which included compensation of £20M for the owners of slaves.

Read this again carefully and *write* a summary of all the important points.

Earl's Story

I live in Toxteth which is in Liverpool. One day I went with my class to visit the Maritime Museum at the Albert Dock. There was a display about the ships taking slaves to the New World and coming back very rich to Liverpool. I felt very sad and very angry as I looked at the pictures. The odd thing is that a lot of the black community in Liverpool now live in houses that were owned by the slavers.

Task 8

Is there a member of your form group (perhaps yourself) or someone in your local community who has Afro-Caribbean ancestry, like Earl? Arrange for someone from the Afro-Caribbean community to speak to your class group or year group, or delegate some members of the class to conduct an interview and then report back. How do black people in the community think and feel about the slave trade?
Do they feel that the attitudes of that time have disappeared or are still to be found in the community?

Extension work

A

Reflect: Why do you think Earl would feel both *sad* and *angry*, while looking at the slave-ship display?

B

Find out about the contribution the black community has made to life in Britain from 1500 up to the present day. (You could write to the Catholic Association for Racial Justice or the Commission for Racial Equality for information. Their addresses can be looked up in a library.)

Rastafarianism

The memory of Africa and the dream of freedom

More about Earl . . .

Earl is actually a Rastafarian, which means that he and his family belong to a religious group of people who follow religious teachings which began in Jamaica. They wear dreadlocks. To understand Rastafarianism, you need to go back in time to a very famous religious leader from Jamaica, Marcus Garvey, who died in 1940. He saw Africa as a symbol of the origins of black people, and going back to Africa was a symbol of black people being set free from poverty and hopelessness.

He said: "It is a decision of the Negro to make Africa a nation to which the Negroes of the world can look for help and support, moral and physical, when ill-treated or abused for being Negroes".

Garvey told his people to: "Look to Africa, when a black king shall be crowned, for the day of deliverance is near".

In November 1930, Ras Tafari was crowned as Emperor of Ethiopia, Haile Selassie I, King of Kings, Lord of Lords. Very soon, many came to believe that he was the living God. Rastafarians believe that the Israelites were black, that Jesus was black, that they are the descendants of the black Israelites, and that God has appeared again in the form of the Emperor king, Haile Selassie, of Ethiopia, a black nation in Africa, the home of black people and the cradle of civilisation. Rastafarians grow their hair in "locks", a symbol of natural life and of the mane of the Lion and of the African warrior, and smoke ganja (marijuana) as an aid to wisdom, prayer and friendship. They think of many parts of western life as Babylon, exile from home in Africa.

There are many Rastafarians like Earl in Britain today, and "reggae" music has been a special way of making their voice heard and celebrating their religious identity. They often wear tams, and the colours red, green and gold.

Task 9

Some people at Earl's school felt that he should not be allowed to wear dreadlocks and a tam. Earl explained it was part of his religion, Rastafarianism, but they did not know much about that so Earl tried to explain . . .

With your partner, role-play the scene.

Extension work

A

Make a list of the main beliefs of Rastafarianism. Use your class or school library to get information.

B

Listen to some songs by the singer, Bob Marley. What are the main themes of his music?

Freedom and rights

Task 10

A Class Project

Choose one or more of the groups mentioned in the boxes below.

PEOPLE NOT FREE TO WORSHIP

WOMEN IN SOCIETY

MIGRANT WORKERS AND THEIR FAMILIES

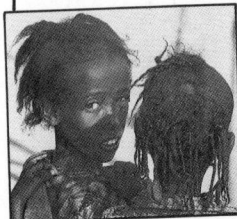

PEOPLE DYING OF HUNGER

REFUGEES OR EXILES

CHILD LABOURERS

THE HOMELESS

?
A GROUP OF YOUR OWN CHOICE

You may decide to choose a group that you are linked with in some way.

e.g. your parents or grandparents may have come from Poland, Ireland, India, the West Indies.

or there may be a group of people in your local community that has a link with one of the groups shown.

or there may be a religious link with one of the groups.

When you have chosen:

Plan how your group will assemble the information you need on this topic.

Decide how your group will present its findings,

e.g. a collage, a playlet, a dance, an assembly, a booklet about . . . etc.

Start with a list of the questions you have about the group you are considering,

e.g. who, where, how long, how many, what problems, how does it feel to be . . . whose fault is it etc.

Concentrate on the group's experience and on understanding its situation, rather than on solutions for the moment.

TIME-LIMIT FOR THIS WORK?

Extension work

A

Present your findings.

B Reflect on the work done.

What sort of feelings do you have as you hear and look at what your class has produced?

Task 11

Plan of Action

In Task 10 you explored the experience of a group of people whose rights and freedoms were under threat or simply denied; you looked for reasons why this was so; and you expressed or presented your ideas.

Now you should reflect on what you have learnt and consider what could be done to change things.

Your plan of action could include:

What *could be* done by:
Governments?
International agencies?
Religious organizations?
Voluntary groups?
School groups and individuals?

What *will be* done by your group?
e.g. A poster about this?
A letter to one of the people with power in this field?
A letter to an organization?
Expressing your support and asking how you could help?
Arranging a brief visit from someone willing to tell your class or year a little more about your chosen topic?

COMIC RELIEF

Extension work

A

Read a booklet about an organization set up to help the people you have been learning about.

B

Compare your *plan of action* with the aims of a voluntary or international group working with the people you have been considering.

How did we do?

Tasks 6–11

1. *What do you know about slavery after studying this section of the module?*
   Do you understand why it was so difficult to have laws passed abolishing it?

2. *Do you understand why the slave trade story continues to be important in Britain and in other parts of the world? How is Rastafarianism linked to this story?*

3. *Did you choose a particular group to study in Task 10?*
   Why did you choose them?
   How do you rate the work you did?

4. *What sort of action did you decide would be effective in Task 11?*
   What was the outcome?

Review of the module

- Describe which part of this module you enjoyed most.
- Look through your work and decide which work in your opinion, is the best. Say why.
- Suggest ways of making this module more interesting.

Hostages, exiles and refugees

Yin escaped by boat from Vietnam with her brother and sister when the war was at its height. Many of the people who escaped by boat were killed by pirate gangs or drowned at sea, but Yin reached safety and came to Britain. She and her family now live in Wales. They had to learn a new language and adapt to living and learning in a new town, and trying to get some qualifications so that they could earn a living.

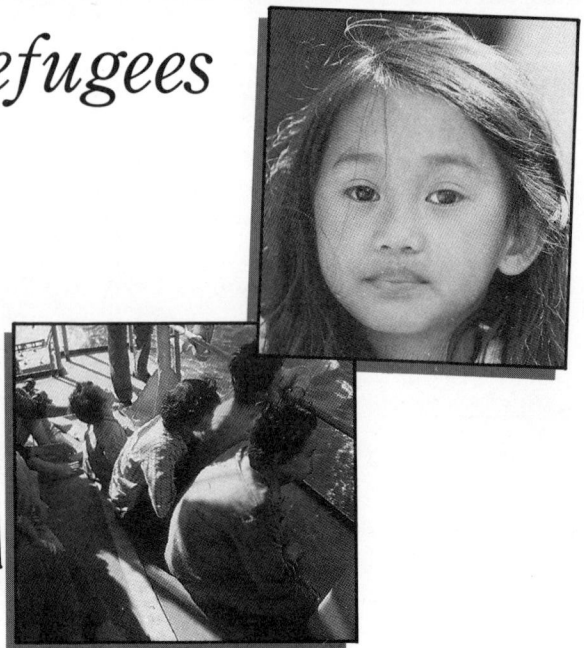

Task 12

Reflect on what it feels like to be a hostage, a refugee or an exile. Find some newspaper cuttings or video news item about someone who has been deprived of freedom in this way. Imagine you are one of these people and tell your story.

Extension work

A

Find out if there is anyone in your family, street or community who has had to flee his or her own country and live in a new country.
Tell the story and *explain* the situation.

B

Discuss with your partner whether taking hostages is a justifiable way of getting people to pay attention to your cause.
What response do you think governments should make in cases like this?

or

Discuss with your partner whether countries should feel a responsibility for accepting exiles and refugees from other countries. *How* would you respond?

The experience of liberation in Judaism

Another word for gaining freedom is Liberation.
You have been looking at different kinds of things from which people want to be liberated.

Liberation can mean gaining:

● Freedom from physical imprisonment/from jail or detention/or exile.

● Freedom from a way of government which is oppressive, which does not allow people basic freedoms. Look back to the beginning of this module and revise your ideas about what basic freedoms everyone should have . . . the right to an education/a home/the right to have a family/a job etc.

● Freedom from drugs or alcohol – many people feel trapped because they are addicted to drugs. Their addiction means that they are not able to be free enough to make choices about what they will do with their lives. The addiction has taken over.

Now you are going to examine the Jewish experience of being liberated.

The Exodus – a story of liberation

Task 13

Trace the main elements of the Exodus story in the Bible. You will find most of it in the second book of the Old Testament called EXODUS, which means the exit or escape from Egypt. If you have already completed the second level module on STORY you will have covered some of this work – do you remember? In this module you will consider and analyse the reasons why and how the Jewish people remember and celebrate their liberation.

Read and Learn About

How the Israelites became slaves in Egypt	Exodus 1:8–14
The birth and childhood of Moses	Exodus 2:1–10
Moses' escape to Midian	Exodus 2:11–15
The burning bush and Moses' mission	Exodus 3:1–12
Moses and Pharaoh	Exodus 5:1–23
The Passover meal	Exodus 12
The Israelites cross the Sea of Reeds	Exodus 14
The song of victory of the Israelites	Exodus 15
The Covenant on Sinai	Exodus 20
Moses' speech to the Israelites	Deuteronomy 30:15–20

Extension work

A

Draw a cartoon of the main events of Moses' life. *Explain* them to your partner.

B

Compose a speech, thanksgiving poem or song for the people of Israel at the time of Moses and the Exodus.

Task 14

Now analyse the Exodus story as a story of liberation.

Can you find any elements in the story which express the experience of people hoping for freedom from various kinds of injustice?

- Migrants
- A minority group
- Slaves
- Exiles
- Refugees
- Persecuted
- Religious minority
- Celebrating the hope of being set free
- Hungry and thirsty

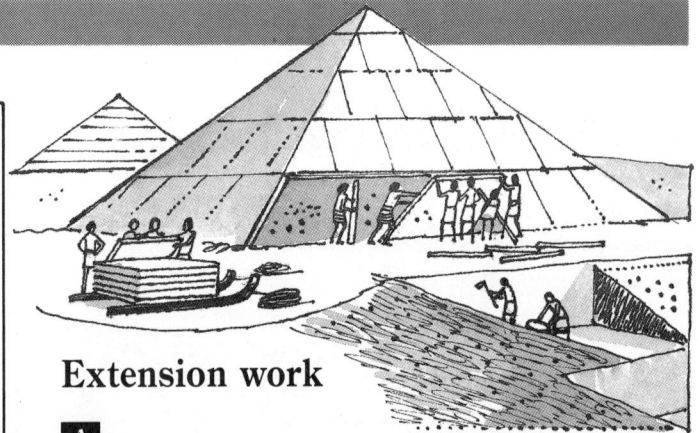

Extension work

A

Write out an example of each experience from the Exodus story.

B

Why has it been important for Jews to remember this experience in their history?

Do you think the group you were learning about in Task 10 could learn anything from the Exodus experience?

Celebrating Pesach in Judaism

Every year Jews celebrate Pesach (Passover) remembering the events of the first Passover and liberation from slavery, and looking forward to happy times in the future.

The Greenberg Family

Harry and Sylvia Greenberg and their daughter and son, Sarah aged 17 and Jacob aged 13, live in Leeds, Yorkshire. In spring, when the feast of Passover is approaching, they make careful preparations for the festival. The house has to be thoroughly cleaned, and all the everyday plates and cutlery put away. During Pesach a special set of crockery, knives, forks and utensils will be used. Any traces of leaven (yeast) such as in breadcrumbs must be cleared away.

On the first evening of Passover, the Greenbergs sit down at table, everybody in their best clothes, for the Pesach Seder (meaning "order" or "arrangement"). The table is set as in the picture. Apart from the candles and cups of wine, there are foods set out on the Seder plate. After the blessing (Kiddush) the symbolic foods are eaten and then it is Jacob's responsibility, as the youngest in the family, to ask four questions which Harry answers by reading from the Haggadah (the story and songs of the Passover). The Greenbergs finish the meal with prayers and songs thanking God for past and present blessings. Jacob remembers how his father used to hide some pieces of matzoth around the house and he used to search for them. Pesach is a very joyful feast and a great family festival for the Jews.

Task 15

Analysing special meals

In the task after this you will be looking more closely at the Seder meal, but first:

Analyse your own experience of special meals.

What special meals have you been involved in? What was being celebrated? Were there any symbols used to express a deeper meaning to the event? Describe the experience . . . and say what it was that made it a special occasion.

Extension work

A

Make a list of the special meals that take place in your local community from time to time.

What sort of things are they intended to celebrate?

B

Compare the Greenberg's celebration of the Seder meal with your experience of a special meal. What similarities and differences are there?

Analysing Pesach

READ the story of the first PASSOVER or LISTEN to a recording of the story on tape (Exodus 12). Now look at the chart below. You will see the main foods and objects which are used as symbols at the Seder meal, and what the symbols mean.

PREPARE a table with the objects and foods used at a Seder meal.

Label each object and attach a card explaining the significance or meaning of each symbol for Jews.

With your partner, test each other by taking it in turns to give the name of a symbol. The partner has to explain how it is used and what it means.

	WINE	For Celebrations.
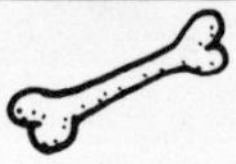	BONE	A symbol of the blood on Hebrews' Houses.
	MATZOH	Bread which has not "risen" like cream crackers.
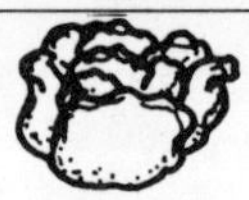	LETTUCE	A sign that there's better food than in Slavery.
	SALT WATER	The tears and sweat of Slavery.
	EGG	The hard times in Egypt. The new life of freedom.
	WATER	To clean hands – no knives/forks.
	HORSE RADISH	Bitter times.
	CANDLE	Jewish faith burns on.
	HAGGADAM	"Telling" the story.
	CHAROSET	Bricks and mortar, built in Slavery.

Extension work

A

Find out if there is a member of the Jewish community who lives locally and who would be willing to come and speak to your class about Pesach.

or

Watch a video of a Seder meal. Look out for the symbols of food on the table, the four cups of wine and the four questions asked by the youngest person present.

What sort of celebration is this?

B

Analyse the blessings and prayers from a Seder meal.

What do they tell you about what the meal is celebrating?

Leader

Now in the presence of loved ones and friends,
before us the emblems of festive rejoicing,
we gather for our sacred celebration.
With the household of Israel, our elders and
young ones,
linking and bonding the past with the future,
we heed once again the divine call
to service.
Living our story that is told for all peoples,
whose shining conclusion is yet to unfold,
we gather to observe the Passover,
as it is written:

Group

You shall keep the Feast of Unleavened Bread,
for on this very day I brought your hosts out of
Egypt. You shall observe this day throughout the
generations as a practice for all times.

Group

This is the bread of affliction,
the poor bread,
which our ancestors ate in the land of Egypt.
Let all who are hungry come and eat.
Let all who are in want
share the hope of Passover.
As we celebrate here,
we join with our people everywhere.
This year we celebrate here,
Next year in the land of Israel.
Now we are all still in bonds.
Next year may all be free.

Now I break the middle *matzah* and conceal one half as the *afikoman*. Later we will share it, as in days of old the Passover offering itself was shared at this service in Jerusalem. Among people everywhere, sharing of bread forms a bond of fellowship. For the sake of our redemption, we say together the ancient words which join us with our own people and with all who are in need, with the wrongly imprisoned and the beggar in the street. For our redemption is bound up with the deliverance from bondage of people everywhere.

Each drop of wine we pour is hope and prayer
that people will cast out the plagues that
threaten everyone
everywhere they are found, beginning in our
own hearts:
    The making of war,
    the teaching of hate and violence,
    despoliation of the earth,
    perversion of justice and of government,
    fomenting of vice and crime,
    neglect of human needs,
    oppression of nations and peoples,
    corruption of culture,
    subjugation of science, learning, and human
    discourse,
    the erosion of freedoms.
We pour ten drops for the plagues upon Egypt.

These selections taken from *A Passover Haggada*:
Central Conference of American Rabbis (Penguin 1982).

Exile and liberation in Judaism

Throughout Jewish history, the experience of being exiled and persecuted and longing to return home has continued to be important for Jews.

- Read Psalm 137 and express in words or movements how the Jewish people felt at that time.
- Play the Boney-M song – "Rivers of Babylon" and compare it with the psalm.

- The Jews were greatly upset by the destruction of the the Temple. Some of their feelings are expressed in a psalm. *Read Psalm 79.*

- Do you know any stories about the sufferings of Jews during the period of the holocaust?

Task 17

Explore and analyse the Jewish experience of exile and return.

THE FIRST EXILE

About 900 years or so BC, the Jewish people was split in two by a civil war, becoming two nations called Israel (in the north) and Judah (in the south). A couple of centuries later, Israel was attacked by the Assyrians who lived in the north, and the people were taken to Assyria where they became part of the Assyrian people and ceased to be a separate nation. About a century later, the Babylonians, an empire in the east, invaded Judah, conquered it, and took the people back to Babylon where they lived in exile until Cyrus, the Emperor of Persia, allowed them to return home.

How did the people feel, taken away to a foreign land, away from their homes and their country, their temple destroyed and the possessions taken?

THE SECOND EXILE – THE DIASPORA

Six hundred years later, the Romans put down a rebellion by the Jews in 70 AD, shortly after the time of Christ. Thousands of Jews were killed, and thousands sent into exile all over the world. The Temple in Jerusalem was destroyed and has never been rebuilt. Today Jews gather and pray at one of the remaining foundation walls of the ancient Temple. This wall is known as "THE WAILING WALL".

THE HOLOCAUST

Nearly 2000 years later, during World War Two, Jews began to be persecuted on a scale never before seen. More than six million Jews were killed in the wholesale destruction or "holocaust" which Adolf Hilter and the Nazis inflicted on the Jewish people.

THE STATE OF ISRAEL

By the end of the war there was a feeling that Jews should have a home country of their own. The United Nations called for the setting up of a new state of Israel. On the 5th May 1948 the new state was ready to provide a new home for many Jewish immigrants. There was much bloodshed in the struggle which took place between those Jews in favour of a new state and Arab people who were settled on the land and other Arab nations. The conflict still goes on.

Photographs of Jerusalem

Places and ceremonies sacred to Christians, Jews and Muslims

● Wailing Wall

● Dome of the Rock

● Holy Sepulchre

Extension work

A

Jerusalem is a special city – "the holy city" – to Christians, Jews and Muslims. Can you *identify* in the photographs places which are special or sacred for these religious traditions? *What* are the people in the photographs celebrating? Do you know why?

B

Why is Jerusalem a special, sacred city to Christians, Jews and Muslims?

What do you think would be the thoughts and feelings of a Christian pilgrim, a Jewish pilgrim or a Muslim pilgrim in the Holy City of Jerusalem on an occasion which is special for each tradition? *Express* those feelings in a diary extract, a poem or a prayer.

ASSESS your work!

Tasks 12–17

1. *Do you know what is meant by*
   (a) an exile? (b) a hostage? (c) a refugee? (d) liberation?

2. *In this section of the module you were looking at how Jews celebrate liberation in the festival of Passover, and particularly in the Seder meal.*
   What are the important elements in the meal?
   Can you recall any of the symbols used?

   Did you read any of the blessings?
   Why is the Passover so important to Jews?

3. *Have you gained an idea of how exile and return have continued to be important to Jews?*
   What was the first exile?
   What was the Diaspora?
   What was the Holocaust?
   Can you remember any of the psalms?

Review of the module

● **How have you fared in this part of the module?**
● **Did you find you were doing good work, learning a lot?**
● **Which parts could have been more interestingly presented, if any?**

The Christian experience of being set free

Good news, good news.

Task 18

Explore your own experience of good news.

Can you think of an occasion when you heard what turned out to be really good news for you?

Write a short story about the experience, showing how the news came, what was good about it, and whether you celebrated this happy occasion in some way.

Communicate your story to the rest of the class, or swop your stories in a group.

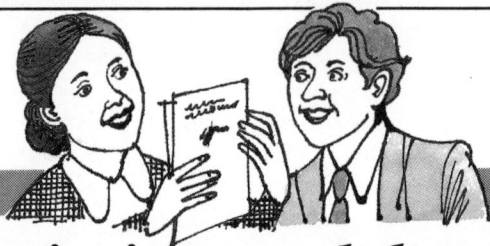

Extension work

A

Think of some occasions when your family or friends have received good news.

How did they react? *Did* they celebrate? *How?*

B

Have there been any occasions that you can remember, or have heard of, when your community (your neighbourhood, district, town) received good news?

Were there celebrations? Do the celebrations continue today? Have the stories about this been written down?

Christians celebrating liberation

Christians believe that Jesus Christ is good news for the world. They believe that, through Jesus, God has made it possible for all people to be set free from the kinds of things that make it difficult for them to live happy and peaceful lives, and so to become close to God and share his life forever. Jesus inspired and challenged people to do this. Some accepted the challenge; some did not!

> He reached the shores of the sea of Galilee, and he went up into the hills. He sat there, and large crowds came to him bringing the lame, the crippled the blind, the dumb and many others; these they put down at his feet and he cured them. The crowds were astonished to see the dumb speaking, the cripples whole again, the lame walking and the blind with sight, and they praised the God of Israel.
>
> Matthew 15:29–31

Task 19

Read the following stories from the gospels and analyse the reactions of people to what JESUS did.

A story of the cure of a deaf man:
Mark 7:31–37
A story of the cure of a man with a withered hand: Matthew 12:9–14
A story of the cure of a paralytic:
Matthew 9:1–8

How would you describe the feelings of the person cured in these stories?
What was the general feeling and reaction of the crowds who witnessed the cures?
Why was the reaction of some Pharisees different?
In what way was Jesus setting people free? From what?

Luke 6:27–38

1. Do you consider this a difficult challenge?
2. If people followed the challenge what
   would they be freed from?
3. What difference would it make if people
   did follow the challenge? Would it be
   "Good news"?

Extension work

A

Draw or *role-play* the reactions of some of the
people in one of the gospel stories you have
just read and studied.

B

Compose a modern version of a gospel story
which challenges people to be set free from the
kind of things that make it difficult for them to
live happy and peaceful lives. *Describe* various
reactions.

**Christians believe that the hopes which are expressed in the Old
Testament are fulfilled in the life, death and resurrection of
Jesus. Christians celebrate these events in a special way during
Holy Week and Easter.**

Task 20

*Explore Christian belief in Jesus, the good news of being set
free and the challenge which this implies.*

The four accounts of Jesus' life are called Gospels. This
word comes from old English words: "good-spell" or "god-
spell" which means "speaking good things" or "good news".
The Greek words "eu angellion" and the Latin word
"evangelium" mean the same thing – good news. That is
where we get the word for a gospel writer – evangelist.

*Your task is to work out why the early Church community
looked on Jesus as being good news for them and why some
people accepted the challenge of being set free while others did
not.*

*A good way to start is to analyse some of the stories which the
evangelists – the "good news writers" – told.*

A forgiveness story:
Luke 15:11–32

1. Why did the younger son
   leave home?
2. What made him change
   his mind and go back
   home? Do you think he
   was set free? From what?
3. Why did his father call for
   a celebration? What kind
   of celebration?
4. Why did the older brother
   not join in the party?

**A story of someone who
found the challenge too hard:**
Mark 10:17–22

1. Why did the young man
   come to Jesus?
2. What was Jesus'
   challenge to him?
3. Why did the young man
   find it hard and go away
   sad?

**The story of someone who
changed his ways:**
Luke 19:1–10

1. Describe Zacchaeus'
   personality.
2. How did he earn his
   living?
3. What did others think of
   him?
4. How did people react to
   Jesus' self invitation to
   Zacchaeus' house?
5. In what way was
   Zacchaeus set free from
   his own selfishness?
6. What was the "good
   news" for other people?

Christians celebrating Holy Week and Easter

Earlier in this module, you were examining how Jews celebrate the experience of being set free and facing the future with hope. In the last task you were exploring how the gospel accounts in Christianity present Jesus as the good news that people are saved from suffering and guilt and living without hope for the future. The gospels lead up to the important events of Holy Week and Easter, which you may have studied in the first celebration module. You may need to RECALL those events now.

You may need to look up the references and read the passages if you are not familiar with them.

Christians celebrate these events during Holy Week and Easter because they believe that they are the way in which Jesus sets humanity free from suffering, failure and death, and makes it possible for people to come really close to God if they choose to respond to him with repentence and faith.

WHAT THE GOSPELS SAY	
PALM SUNDAY Jesus enters Jerusalem to a hero's welcome *Mark 11:1–10*	**MAUNDY THURSDAY** Jesus shares the last supper with his friends *Mark 14:12–25*
GOOD FRIDAY Jesus is crucified, dies and is buried *Mark 14: 32 – 15: 47*	**EASTER SUNDAY** Jesus overcomes sin and death by rising from the dead *Mark 16:1–8*

Task 21

Examine the pictures of Christians celebrating Holy Week and Easter and try to explain how each picture shows Christians celebrating that Jesus is their liberator or saviour.

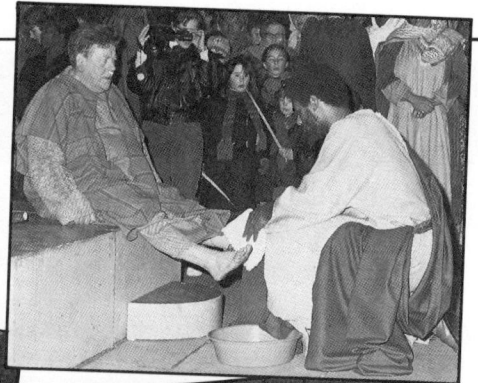

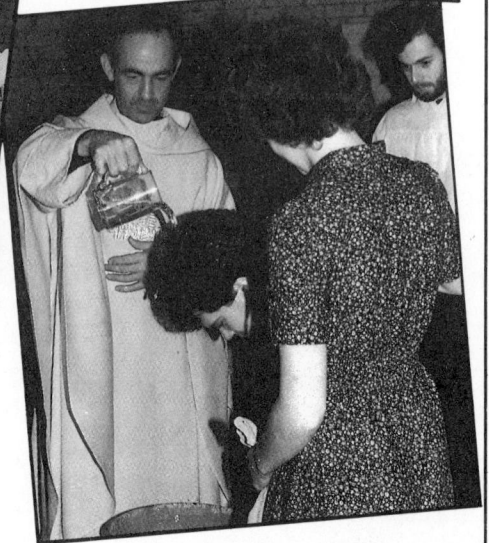

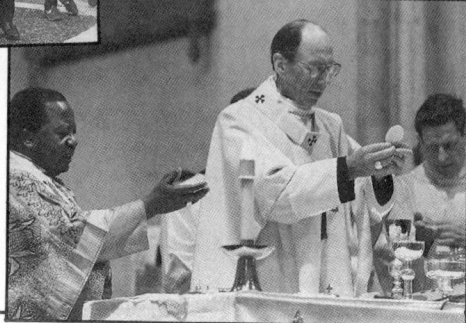

46

PRAYERS AND BLESSINGS FROM ROMAN CATHOLIC LITURGY

Today we honour Christ our triumphant King
by carrying these branches.
May we honour you every day
by living always in him,
for he is Lord for ever and ever.

(Blessing of palms)

Where charity and love are found, there is
God.
Therefore when we are together,
let us take heed not to be divided in mind.
Let there be an end to bitterness and
quarrels, an end to strife,
and in our midst be Christ our God.

(Antiphon during Washing of Feet, Holy Thursday)

Lord, by your cross and resurrection
you have set us free.
You are the Saviour of the world.

(Acclamation after consecration)

The Father of mercies has given us an
example of unselfish love
in the sufferings of his only Son.
Through your service of God and neighbour
may you receive his countless blessings.

(Final blessing, Passion Sunday)

Through the resurrection of his Son
God has redeemed you and made you his
children.
May he bless you with joy. Amen

The Redeemer has given you lasting
freedom.
May you inherit his everlasting life. Amen

By faith you rose with him in baptism
May your lives be holy,
so that you will be united with him for ever.

Amen
(Final blessing during Easter season)

Lord, may this sacrifice,
which has made our peace with you,
advance the peace and salvation of all the
world.
Strengthen in faith and love your pilgrim
Church on earth . . .

(From the third Eucharistic Prayer)

Extension work

A

Choose one of the events of Holy Week and Easter and use *movement* or *dance* to express what it means for Christians.

B

Are there any SYMBOLS in the pictures which *show* that Christians want to follow the example of Jesus? In what way? How do the prayers *show* this?

Write a prayer, antiphon, hymn or blessing which you consider appropriate for a Christian celebration of one of the days of Holy Week.

Christians celebrating the Eucharist

When Christians celebrate the special meal which is called EUCHARIST (which means Thanksgiving) they are celebrating in the way that Jesus celebrated the Passover as the Last Supper before his death. They also celebrate the sacrifice of Jesus on the cross because they believe that in sacrificing himself out of love Jesus conquered death and rose again. In the Eucharist Christians celebrate their belief that Jesus continues to be present in his community, especially when they gather together to pray, to listen to the Word of God in scriptures, and when they receive the consecrated bread and wine – the body and blood of Christ. They give thanks for the sacrifice of Jesus and are helped and strengthened to live in his way.

Task 22

Read these accounts of the Last Supper:

| John 13:1–15 | Luke 22:7–20 |

Can you find the link with:
- the Passover?
- the death of Jesus?
- Christians continuing to celebrate the Eucharist?

Find and copy out the words of Jesus at the Last Supper which are said during a celebration of the Eucharist today.

Explain what you think the symbols of:
    breaking bread
    pouring wine
    sharing a meal
might be expressing. (Remember the link with what you have been studying in the module.)

For Christians the Eucharist is not just about remembering the actions Jesus did a long time ago. The Eucharist is also a challenge to live the way of Jesus today.

The Eucharist feeds Christians for their journey through life.
As Christians are fed so they are also called to feed the hungry of the world. This means sharing not just food, but also resources. When Christians celebrate the Eucharist it is not as escape from life, it is a way of being strengthened to live life more fully.

What do you think it might mean in practice for Christians to be "broken and shared out" in the service of other people?
Can you find some examples of people who have spent themselves in helping others to be free of pain, guilt, sickness or poverty? Perhaps there are people you know in your family or local community who do this, as well as famous people.

Extension work

A

Make a collage of the symbols used in a Christian Eucharist and *explain* what they might be saying about being set free.

B

Compare a celebration of the Eucharist with the Seder meal in a Jewish Passover festival. *List* the similarities and differences and *analyse* the connection between these two religious celebrations.

Taking responsibility

Many Christians believe not just that Jesus has set people free to be with God forever, but that he is part of their struggle to be free human beings now; free to make choices and to have dignity and self-respect, and a fair share of the resources needed for a happy life. They believe that Jesus has given them the freedom to take responsibility for how they live.

Most of the world's Christians live in the southern hemisphere where the struggle to be free is something people are very aware of.
People like Pilar Alvarez who lives in Brazil:

Let me tell you what being a Christian means to me.

In my town, everyone is poor and we have never owned any of the land we work on BUT we do live as a community, including meeting together to read and learn and to work out how we should live.

Reading about Jesus in the Bible has helped us to begin to take more responsiblity for each other and to struggle against some of the injustice we face.

We have organized our own weaving cooperative, we look after the widows and the orphaned children in our part of the parish, and we make sure that we get fair prices for the vegetables we grow.

The way Jesus gave himself for the poor and the downtrodden people gives us strength to struggle for our rights and a just way of life. We've got every reason to celebrate now, but we also look forward in hope for the future.

Task 23

Compare what Pilar and her community are doing with what you are doing in your R.E. programme.

Pilar and her community are:

- Thinking about their own experience of life.
- Trying to understand why things are the way they are.

- Reflecting on a religious view of life and what might be learned.
- Taking responsibility for living life in the way they feel is right.

How does that compare with the way that you are growing and learning? Do you feel that you are being encouraged to learn and reflect and take responsibility?

Extension work

A

Compare Pilar's church community with a parish, local church or other religious group that you know. What *similarities* and *differences* are there?

B

What have you *learned* from doing this module which might help you to work out a good way to use whatever freedom you have?

ASSESS your work!

Tasks 18–23

1. *In Task 18 you were exploring your experience of getting good news. What was the connection between that task and Task 20?*

2. *What sense does it make to call Good Friday and Easter celebrations? Why do Christians continue to celebrate this festival?*

3. *What links can you find, and what differences, between the Jewish celebration of*

Passover and Christian celebration of Eucharist?

4. *Why do some Christians feel they should have a special commitment to the poor?*

What progress do you think you have made in this part of the module? What did you find easy to do, more difficult, interesting? How might it have been made more interesting?

Review of the module

What have been your successes in your work in this module?

How do you think you could improve your work?

Have you enjoyed your work?

We are the Champions!

Were you
1. Usually on time for class/usually late for class?
2. Hardworking . . . most of the time/some of the time/not very often?
3. Able to work by yourself sometimes?
4. Able to work with others in a group?

Did you
5. Find the work very easy or very difficult?
6. Work when the teacher was busy with other people or only when the teacher was with you?
7. Cooperate with the teacher?
8. Did you follow up any of the work you did at home by reading or finding out more about any of the topics you have covered?
9. Did you do any extension/project work?

Do you
10. Find it easy to tell the teacher of any problems you had?
11. Prefer to work by yourself or with others?

Now, share what you have done with your class teacher.

Congratulations! You have completed *Celebration*. Well done! Feel free to celebrate!

This module of work in your R.E. programme is called

Values Level Two

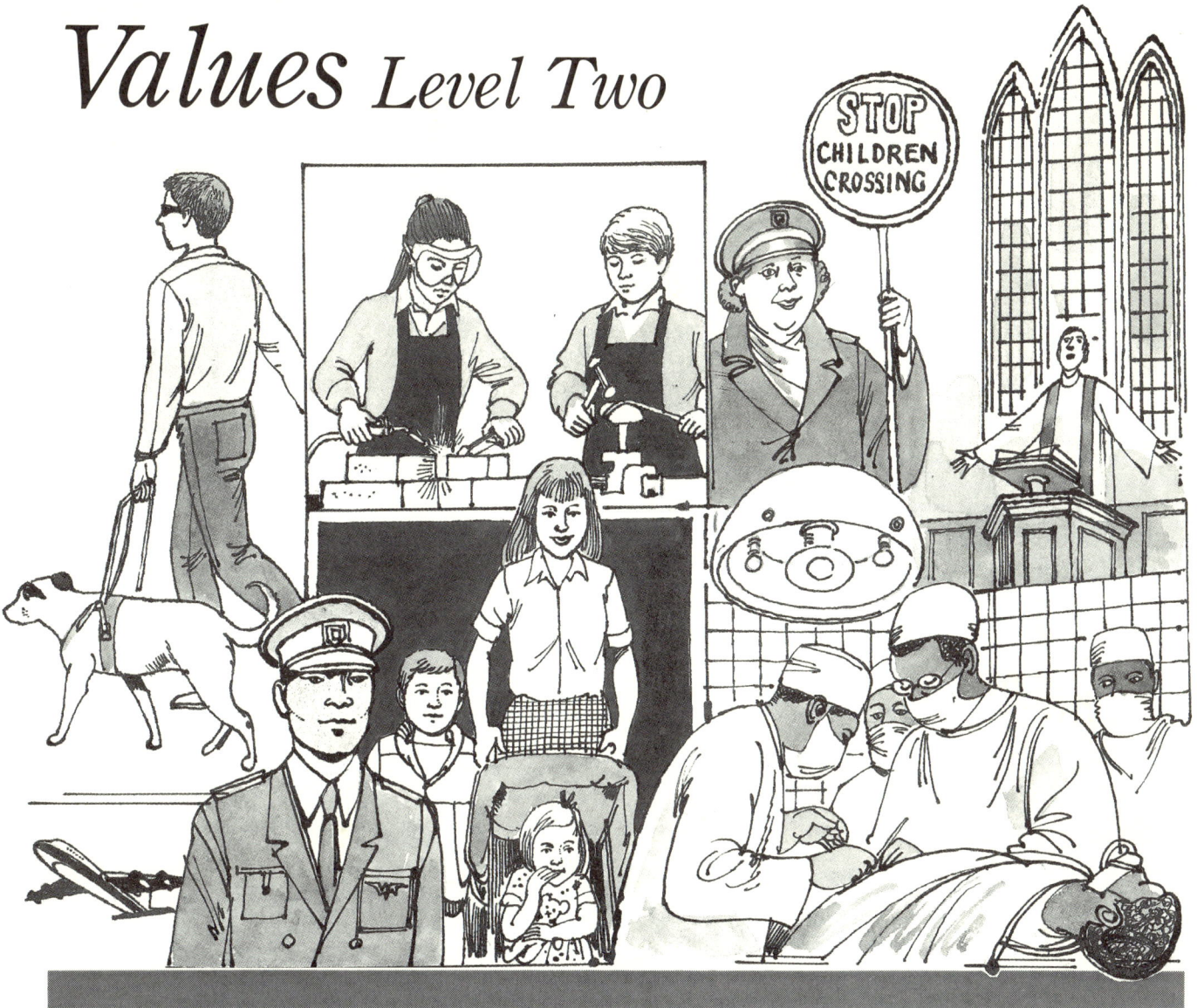

It is all about how values are related to the responsibilities which people have, and especially about the values which people recognize as important in being responsible members of the Christian and Jewish traditions.

Here are some of the activities you will be involved in for this module:

- **describing and analysing** your experience of making decisions.

- **exploring and defining** what you need and what you want.

- **analysing** right and wrong choices.

- **tracing** the possible outcomes of choices.

- **exploring** the links between freedom and responsibility.

- **considering** the role of conscience.

- **investigating** power, leadership and service in your local community and in school.

- **understanding** the notion of responsibility in Judaism.

- **examining** the Christian view of responsibility for self, others and the world.

- **reflecting** on how life for boys and girls in Third World countries is affected by decisions made in the more affluent nations.

51

RECALL

If you have already studied the Values module at Level One, then you should spend a little time recalling your work in that module. Look through your file or work book and see what was involved in exploring values . . .

Do you recall exploring:

- personal values?
- attitudes?
- decisions and choices?
- priorities

Do you recall doing a project on values in your school and in your local community?

Do you recall investigating values in the media and the world of "pop"?

Do you recall exploring values in an Indian village school and in the Hindu community?

Do you recall studying Christian values in the life of Jesus and in relations between the churches?

Finally, from your own review of progress in the Values module at Level One, what particular aspect of your work would you hope to improve on in this module?

The first few tasks of this module overlap with the work covered at Level One. Just before you start, there are two things you should do:

FIRST: Look at the list of activities and see how they are linked to the four strands of your experience which *Weaving the Web* deals with.

You will notice that where Values Level One emphasized **describing** your experience, at Level Two, the emphasis is on **analysing** and **understanding** roles and responsibilities.

SECOND: Some of the work for this module needs to be planned for now. Your teacher will help you to do this.

READY? Good. Now lets get weaving on . . . *Values, Level Two*

Decisions? Decisions!

Being able to make your own decisions is an important part of being YOU.

Just think of all the choices you make over a period of time:

- What shall I do next?
- What should I wear?
- Who will I sit next to?
- What time should I leave?
- Where should I go?
- What shall I eat?
- Whom will I have for a friend?
- Which of my friends should I spend most time with?
- Which book shall I read?

- What sport or hobby will I choose?
- Should I talk over this particular problem with somebody?
- Should I ask permission to do this or not?
- What options should I choose for next year?
- What do I want to be?
- How should I react when . . . ?
- What will I say if . . . ?

Task 1

By yourself:

Check how many of these decisions you have been involved in making yourself.

Add to the list any more decisions or choices you have been faced with – you can express these very generally if you feel they may be too personal to be detailed.

With your partner:

Compare: whether your lists are the same or different.

Discuss: which of the decisions are most difficult.

Decide: whether you are generally faced with very similar or very different kinds of decisions, or find that the same or different decisions are difficult for each of you.

GROUP WORK:

Consider: what would be the best way to find out whether all your class are involved in making similar or very different decisions? Your teacher will help to arrange this.
Remember: some people may decide that some decisions are a little too personal to be discussed openly in class.

Draw some conclusions from your discussion and record or display them.

Extension work

A

Make up a story about someone faced with a difficult choice, and *either* write or draw the story in your file or notebooks, *or* record it on tape.

B

You may feel that different kinds of choices have to be made at different stages in life. *Map out* what you feel are the kind of choices typically made at various stages.

For example:
- infancy
- childhood
- adolescence
- young adulthood
- middle age
- later life

Freedom: the power to choose

What would it be like to be unable to make some basic decisions and choices, such as:

To choose what music you listen to.

To be able to choose to give an opinion openly (to say what you think).

To choose to go where you like on holiday.

To live by what you believe in *or* to act in accordance with your beliefs.

To choose what you will aim to be when you leave school.

Task 2 GROUP WORK

Role-play a situation where somebody is being deprived of the freedom to make a decision. You may wish to choose one of the freedoms mentioned or to pick your own.

Analyse the situation you have role-played. What was at stake?
What did it feel like to be deprived of the power to choose?
Did someone want to remove that freedom? Or were the circumstances stopping free choice?
What did the person do to try to secure his/her freedom of choice?

Extension work

A

Find and *display* some photographs from newspapers or magazines, showing people who have been deprived of the freedoms mentioned at the beginning of this task.
Create a dance to express what the people involved might be feeling.

B

Find out about a real situation in the news today or recently, where the freedom to make a basic decision or choice about life is in question.
Use the questions in Task 2 (Analyse) to *write* about it.

Moral choices: choosing right or wrong

Task 3

A Case Study:

Laura is 12. She would like her own stereo-cassette player, but her parents have not been able to find the money yet to buy her one. Then, one day . . .

> **A principle** is a basic ground rule for deciding what is the right thing to do. Some people may accept different principles from other people.

GROUP WORK

List: the possible reasons Laura might give for taking the stereo.

List: the possible reasons Laura might give for NOT taking the stereo.

Decide: what you think is the RIGHT thing for Laura to do, and say **Why**?

Analyse: the reasons for the decision you have made.

Which principle was your group working on in reaching its decision?

What do you think might happen (what would be the **consequences**) if everyone in the world agreed to base their choices on the principle chosen by your group?

Reflect

What do you personally think about the moral choice facing Laura?
How would you react to someone who took your belongings without your permission?

Role-play

Laura decides to take the stereo while nobody is looking. She puts it in her bedroom. At teatime her father asks who she has borrowed the stereo from.

Extension work

A

A MORAL choice is to do with deciding what is the right or wrong thing to do.
Describe a TV film, or play, or book where the characters faced a moral choice. *Identify* the principle on which their decision was based.

B

Write an imaginative story about someone who has to decide what is the right thing to do in a certain situation. Your story should show clearly the principle on which the decision is made.

Needs and wants

When you are making your choices, you may sometimes have to decide what you really want.

Task 4

The Lotsawants Delivery Service guarantees to deliver to your door all the things you want in life.

Copy the form into your file or workbook and fill it in. Compare your wishes with your partner.

GROUP WORK
Your group is a company which advises people on what they need for a happy life. Your task is to compose a letter to a client who has written for advice on what is needed for a happy life.

Extension work

ALL-U-NEED CO. LTD.

Dear Client,
    We would like to advise you that all you need for a happy life is . . .

_____
_____
_____

Yours sincerely
ALL-U-NEED Co. Ltd.

A

Interview some members of your community about what they _want most_ out of life, and about what they feel they really _need_ for a happy life.

B

Is there any difference between what people say they _want_ and what they feel they _need_ for a happy life? Buddhists believe that suffering in life is caused by people _wanting_ or _craving_. What do you feel about this?

Influences

The choices we make, our values and our views, are often influenced by other people.

Task 5

Fill in the chart in your file or workbook.

In your choice of . . .	Who or what has influenced you most?
Clothes	
Hobbies	
Music	
Food in the school cafeteria	
Hairstyle	
How you spend free time	
Books you read	
Programmes you watch	
Clubs you belong to	

In your views about . . .	Who has influenced you most?
Sport	
Politics	
Religion	
School	
Environment	
War	
The law	

Analyse which are the strongest influences on your choices and views.

Consequences

Part of what needs to be taken into account when making decisions and choices is what *will* happen or what *could* happen as a result of your choice. Some of the **consequences** of a decision or choice could be good or desirable, whilst other consquences could be bad, even disastrous.

Extension work

A

Role-play a situation where someone's choice is strongly influenced by what other people do or say.

B

A **pressure group** is a group which sets out to try to have a strong influence on a decision which is about to be made.

Find an example of this in your local community or in the news. *What* does this pressure group want and *how* does it go about achieving its aim?

Task 6

With your partner, trace the possible consequences of the following decisions or choices.

You and your friends vandalise a phone box.

You let down the tyres of a car.

You do a sponsored run for charity.

You agree to do the shopping every evening for an elderly neighbour.

You play near a railway line.

You set off the school fire alarm for a joke.

You break a street light with a stone.

You accept the job of team captain.

*In view of the **consequences**, what do you think of the decision?*

Extension work

A GROUP WORK

Everyone in the group makes one or two cards with situations on. The cards are then pooled and shuffled and placed face down. Each member of the group takes it in turn to pick up a card and **analyse** the possible consequences of the choice or decision on the card.

B

Write an imaginative short story with the theme **Ignoring the Consequences**

Conscience

the power to judge what is right or wrong

You have been looking at different aspects of making choices:

- Types of choices.
- Being free to choose.
- Moral choices and principles.
- Needs and wants.
- Influences.
- Consequences.

Now you are going to explore the power which human beings have to judge which actions are right and which are wrong. This power or capacity for making moral judgements is called CONSCIENCE. Like all capacities or skills, it can be better developed or less well developed in different people.

Extension work

A

Give an example of a time when you had to judge whether something you were going to do was right or wrong.
How did you decide?

B

Research and *analyse* what is meant by:
A Conscientious Objector
A Prisoner of Conscience

Find an example of each
or
Find out about the work of Amnesty International

Task 7 — GROUP WORK

Look at the examples below and, in your group, discuss how well developed you think the conscience of each person is.

"I don't break things, because Mummy gets angry if I do."

"Don't do that – it's not fair."

"Well, nobody got hurt, did they?"

"I wouldn't do that because I wouldn't like it if anyone did that to me."

"It must be OK – all my friends did the same!"

Which is the most developed conscience?/Why?

Your **Conscience**, or your ability to judge right and wrong, may be at work *before* or *after* you decide to take an action, but people don't always actually *do* what they think is *right*.

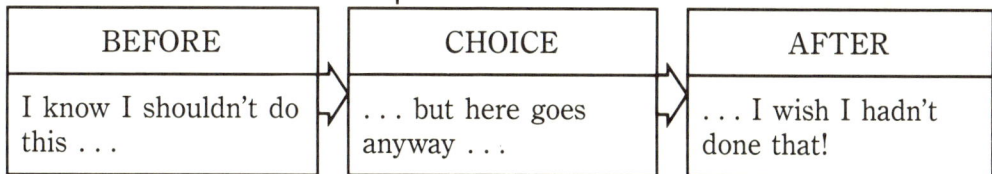

BEFORE	CHOICE	AFTER
I know I shouldn't do this . . .	. . . but here goes anyway . . .	. . . I wish I hadn't done that!

Has this ever happened to you?

What is meant by an "uneasy conscience"?

Can you think of an example of how religious beliefs help people decide what is right and wrong? In what ways should the moral teachings of Jesus and the Church influence the decisions of Christians? Do your religious beliefs help and influence your decisions?

Taking responsibility

To be responsible literally means to be answerable for the decisions and choices you make. The more decisions and choices you are free to make about your own life, the more responsibility you take on.

Task 8

With your partner, fill in the chart in your file or workbook.

	Decisions or choices made	Amount of responsibility	How much responsibility left to parents
babies			
7–8 years			
12–13 years			
adults			

Extension work

A

Make a list of your responsibilities
Which are the most serious ones?

B

Analyse the responsibilities people usually get at the various stages of life.

Pool the ideas in your class group and collect and display them in one large chart. Find a way of showing how freedom relates to responsibilities.

ASSESS your work!

Tasks 1–8

1. *Did you explore the kinds of decisions people in your class group are involved in making?*
   What did you discover? What makes a decision a difficult one?

2. *Why is freedom valued and fought for? Did you find some examples of people fighting for the right to be able to make decisions for themselves?*

3. *What do people in your age group think about stealing?*
   What did you learn about the principles people work on when making moral choices?

4. *Is there anything that people need for a happy life, do you think? Are your views the same or different from those of your friends?*

5. *What did you find are the strongest influences on young people?*

6. *Can you explain what is meant by the consequences of an action?*

7. *What do people mean when they speak of conscience?*

8. *What did your class conclude about the responsibilities that people have?*

9. *How much of the extension work did you manage?*

10. *Which of the tasks did you enjoy most?*

Looking at power

Task 9 — Brainstorming

How many types of POWER can you think of?
Here are a few examples to get you started:

NOW: For each of the examples of power, analyse its use and effects and list them.

ELECTRICAL POWER

MUSCLE POWER

SUPER-POWER

BRAIN POWER

POWER	USE	EFFECTS
Light Bulb	In house, street, car, factory, stadium, etc.	Give light, warning signal, etc.
Muscle	In different parts of body where leverage or movement needed	Lifting, moving, hitting, throwing, etc.

Extension work

A

Choose one of your examples of power and design a set of movements or a dance to express an aspect of "power" and its use.

B Reflect and Evaluate

Look at your list of "powers" and their uses and effects.
Think about how each kind of power is used.
Evaluate the use of each kind of power – what do you think is a positive, good use of that power?
What do you think would be a *misuse* or *abuse* of that power?
Say why and give some examples.

Power in the community

Task 10

Answer the questions in each section.

In the last task, you were exploring different kinds of power. Some of the examples you were given were of a kind of power that you might explore in your science lessons.

e.g. electricity, horse power, fire-power,
wave-power, muscle power.

PHYSICAL POWER

It includes the power that can be found in the physical resources of the world, some of which can be harnessed for our use and some which we may never succeed in taming, for example, lightning, volcanoes.

Did you find your own examples of physical power when you were "brainstorming"?
Can you think of any more?

How many of your examples were to do with power that **people** have (some of it is included in physical power)?

Here we could include:

| PROPERTY POWER |

—the power that comes with being wealthy or owning land and property.

| ROLE POWER |

—the kind of power you have because other people have given it to you, for example:

Captain of a team, prefect, prime minister, chairperson, representative, supervisor.

It is the power that comes with the **role** that you play, or the **position** you hold.

Did you find examples of **role power** in your "brainstorming"?

| POWER GAINED FROM PERSONAL EXPERIENCE |

This includes:
Knowledge you have acquired.
Skills you have developed.
Experiences you have had.
Wisdom you have gained.
Expertise you have (being recognized as being good at something).

e.g. what sort of knowledge, skill and expertise is needed to be recognized as:
- A good driving instructor?
- A good cook?
- A good student?
- A good teacher?
- A good parent?
- A good team coach?
- A good factory manager?

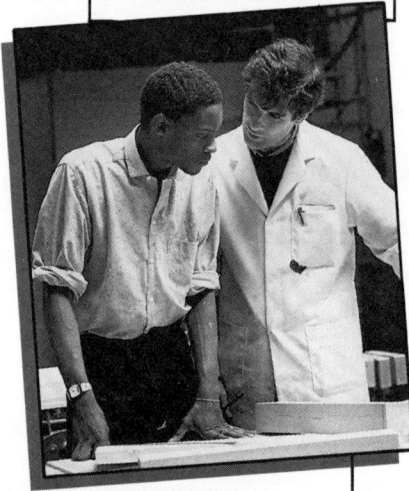

What sort of power is this – what does it depend on?
(Clue – look at the description of **expertise** above.)

| PERSONALITY POWER |

Lots of people have a great deal of power and influence without being in an official position or an expert.

Think of someone you know who can influence others because of being:
- A good talker?
- A good listener?
- Personally attractive?
- Reliable?
- Fun to be with?
- Very determined?
- Disabled, coping well?
- Well-liked or respected?
- A strong character?

| GROUP POWER |

Groups usually exercise power that the individuals in them could not. The group depends on the powers that individuals bring to it, but combines the power.

What powers do the groups below have that the individuals in them normally don't?

a military power

a political party

an alliance of nations

a union

a religious community

a netball team

a committee

a gang

a welfare state (society where basic needs are provided for)

SPIRITUAL POWER

Some people have power to inspire others by what they say or do. They encourage, challenge, enlighten or give a lead to other people in reflecting on life and how to live. They help others to find and experience meaning, purpose and value in life. This is usually thought of as the "spiritual" dimension of life. People may inspire others through music, art, architecture, brave deeds, response to suffering and in many other ways. In religion, people may be inspired to discover God or to search for lasting happiness.

Look at the list below and think of some examples of people, either famous or everyday members of your community, who inspire others to reflect on and respond to life in the deepest way:
e.g. a great saint, prophet, guru, leader, teacher, artist, musician, writer, poet, heroic figure, member of your local or national community or religious tradition, whose work is an inspiration to others or may be thought of as a strong spiritual influence.

Project

Look at your local community (your town or neighbourhood) and try to answer the following questions about it:

PHYSICAL POWER
Who in your community is strong because of their physical presence?

PERSONALITY POWER
Who is influential by virtue of being a strong personality?

PROPERTY POWER
Who in your community is influential because of wealth or property?

GROUP POWER
What powerful groups are there in your community?

ROLE POWER
Who is influential because of the position they hold?

SPIRITUAL POWER
Are there any strong spiritual influences in your community?

EXPERIENCE POWER
Who is recognized for the skills, knowledge or expertise they have?

Extension work

A and **B**
EXPLAIN how you would change/seek to improve things in your local community.

Leadership and service in the community

Earlier in the module you looked at the idea that the more decisions you are able to make for yourself, the more responsibility you take on. In this task you are going to look at the responsibilities which are taken on by the leaders of the groups or local community that you belong to.

Here are two views of leadership and power:

> Leadership is about being in charge and getting your own way by making everyone else do just what you want. They put you there because you know best!

> Leadership is about taking responsibility, making wise decisions, and taking a lead in serving the members of the community in whatever way is best.

Task 11

Analyse the leadership in your local community, your town, your club, your parish, your neighbourhood. Which of the views above most nearly reflects how your leaders see their task?

Present evidence for your views in as balanced and as fair a way as you can.

Extension work

A

Invite a community leader to your class and put your views to him or her.

B

Reflect on how your visitor responded and *write* your reaction to and evaluation of the response.

Leadership, and service in school

Task 12

In this task you are invited to analyse what makes for good leadership, in your school, and how the needs of all who are part of the school community are best served.

Based on your experience, analyse the qualities, the kind of leadership, that would best serve your school, that you would look for in your ideal:
- Classteacher.
- Prefect.
- Caretaker.
- Pupil.

Extension work

A

Role-play a situation where good leadership is being exercised in your school.

B

Write a letter to the prefects praising good aspects of their leadership and suggesting how other aspects could be improved.

Communal responsibility

In the last task you were analysing how people take responsibility in your school community. This task looks a little wider – at the idea that when you belong to a community you share some responsibility together for its successes and failures.

Task 13

Analysing community service in school.

Identify the positive contributions which members of your school make to the local community.
How are people in your neighbourhood served by your school?
What features of life in your local community do members of your school take a lead in promoting?

Identify the less positive aspects of how members of your school community influence your neighbourhood.
How does this reflect on the whole school?
What image of your school does this create?

Reflect: Does the image of your school matter?
What could your class do to help create more positive attitudes in school towards the local community?

Extension work

A

Prepare a series of *movements* or *dance* set to music, expressing the idea of group or communal responsibility.

B

Write in your group a short dramatic piece for presentation, about an issue where members of your school could be making a more positive contribution to the local community.

ASSESS your work! Tasks 9–13

1. *How many examples of power did you think of?*
   What is power?
2. *In Task 10 you looked at some kinds of power in more detail.*
   Did you do the project about power in the local community?
   What did you learn from this?
3. *What makes for a good leader in your view?*
   Did you find some examples of good leadership in your local community?
4. *Did you find Task 12 easy or difficult to do? Say why.*
5. *Can you give an example of communal or group responsibility?*
   What did you learn about this in Task 13?

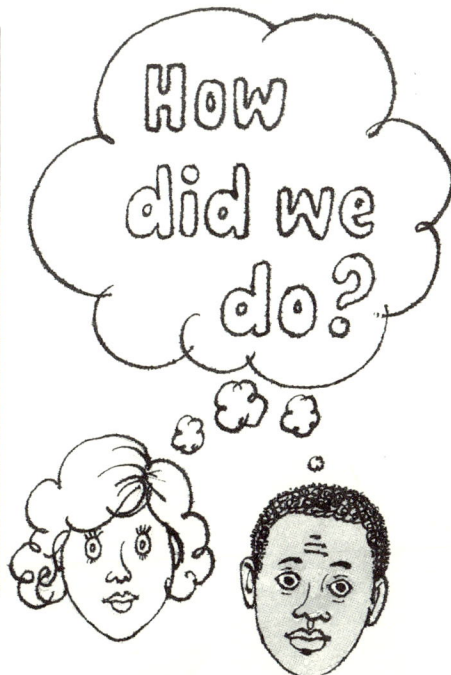

So far in this module you have been working on three aspects of
Values
        . . . How choices are made.
        . . . What responsibility is.
        . . . How authority, power and leadership are exercised.

You are now going to examine these aspects of values within the Jewish tradition.

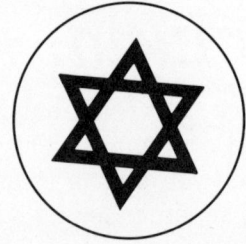

Authority and leadership in Judaism

Meet Elana.

Elana is thirteen and lives in London. She is Jewish.
In school, she has been making a study of some of the first leaders of the Jewish people.
Here is a page from her school workbook. . .

Saul, the first king of Israel

The people of Israel began to want a leader like other nations. Samuel said this was not a good idea but in the end he made Saul the first king of the Israelites.

At first Saul was very successful and won many battles but later he became power mad and very jealous, and he tried to kill David.

In time he went off his head and the people did not want him anymore as king.

✓ Good work, Elana.

Task 14

This story from the first book of Samuel shows how power can corrupt a leader and cause misery for people.

Reflection

Can you think of any ways that you have changed for better or worse during this year?

Can you think of any people in modern times who have misused their power or acted irresponsibly so that their nation suffered?

There are other leaders in the history of the Jewish people who are revered as very great and very wise leaders, although they did not do everything right. The Bible does not try to hide the problems that David and his son, Solomon, for example, had in being king.

Now, can you help Elana with her homework? She has been asked to investigate why King David is an important figure in Jewish history, even for Jews today. You might do this by compiling a dosier on David, starting with the stories in
2 Samuel 5–8
2 Samuel 11–12

> The King David File:
> Portrait of a Leader

You could call this and find a way of displaying your work in the classroom.

Extension work

A

Compose an imaginative life story of King David in words or pictures, or on tape. *Decide* whether you think he was **always** a good and wise leader.

B Research:

Find out about how the Jewish communities around the world are organized.
Who are the leaders of the Jewish community in your country?
How influential are these leaders in the life of the community in your country?

Responsibility in Judaism

It is only a year since Elana's sister, Rachel, was married.
At the time Elana was doing some work in school about the responsibilities that are part of being a member of the Jewish tradition. While she was at her sister's wedding, Elana had an idea how she could do her project on "responsibilities". She drew the main objects used at Rachel's wedding to point to the **values** that Jews hold.

Where the Rabbi reads the blessing and reminds the couple of their responsibilities in marriage.

Chuppah (canopy)
Closed on top: symbol of the close family life of a Jewish family.

Open sides: a symbol of the welcome always available to friends and the community.

Symbol of a new home, homes being the centre of Jewish life and worship.

KETUBAH or contract

Wine is used often by Jews when asking for God's blessing.

Cups of Wine

A symbol of the covenant being made and a sign of the covenant between God and his people.

the ring

Like a link in a chain, the chain of all the generations in Judaism.

The seven blessings symbolise the seven days of creation, to which marriage is compared.

A wine glass is crushed under the bridegroom's heel – a sign of the difficulties of married life and a reminder of Jewish suffering and the destruction of the Temple.

Elana then showed how each of the main responsibilities and values in Judaism had been pointed to in the ceremony:
● To worship the one, true God.
● To live according to the covenant (Torah).
● To value the home as a spiritual centre for family life and bringing up children in the faith and practice of Judaism.

● To observe the Sabbath and important rituals, festivals, and dietary laws of the Jewish tradition.
● To give an example to the world of how God would like us to live.
● To care for the world which God has created and given to mankind.

Task 15

Make models of the main objects used at a Jewish wedding ceremony and write a short commentary to show how they illustrate the main values and responsibilities for Jews today.

Extension work

A

Read the Creation stories in Genesis Chapters 1 & 2 and the Ten Commandments in Exodus 20, and *pick out* any words which deal with **responsibility.**

B

Write a short pen-portrait about a prominent Jewish figure in your country who has championed certain values:
e.g. Immanuel Jackobovits
      Julia Neuberger
      Lionel Blue

Say how you feel they have *influenced* people in this country.

66

Choosing where to live – the Refuseniks

Task 16

Read the following story about Anatoly Scharansky and identify the values which he hoped to find in Israel that he felt were not possible at that time in the USSR.

Anatoly Scharansky lived in Russia. Anatoly was of Jewish descent and very aware of the cruel way that Jews in eastern Europe, as well as in Germany, had been treated. He protested about the way that people in Russia were not free to speak their minds openly, or to worship freely if they wanted to, or to get information about other parts of the world through newspapers or television. He was specially concerned about the lack of freedom to emigrate from Russia and be reunited with other members of the family in other countries. Anatoly's wife was in Israel, but he was not allowed to join her and he and many others who complained about their rights were treated harshly and often imprisoned.

Anatoly used to read the story of the Exodus and he began to identify with the people of the first passover, longing for freedom in a new land. Eventually after much campaigning by people around the world, including his wife, Anatoly Scharansky was set free in Berlin in 1986 and joined his wife in Israel. Soon after this, the Soviet authorities began to relax some of the tight controls on freedom that Scharansky and others had complained about, and the policy of "glasnost", moving towards a more free and open society, became an official policy in the USSR.

Extension work

A

Role-play a situation where you are applying for permission to emigrate to a country which you feel has values closer to yours than where you live now.

B Research

The state of Israel was founded in 1948.
Find out a little about:
(a) the tension between religious and secular values.
(b) the tension between different religious groups.

ASSESS your work!

How did we do?

Tasks 14–16

1. *Why are Saul, David and Solomon important for Jews today? What did you find out about Jews who give a lead in public life today?*
2. *What are the main religious values of the Jewish community? How are these values symbolized in a wedding ceremony?*
3. *Did you manage any of the extension work after the story of Anatoly Scharansky?*

You have been assessing your progress in learning about the values which members of the Jewish faith aspire to. In the next section of the module you will be trying to understand the values involved in the Christian view of responsibility.

Christian responsibility: responsibility for your whole self

In this section of the module you will consider some aspects of Christian responsibility. Christians believe that in Jesus, God shows ("reveals") how people should live their lives. They believe that if they try to be and act like Jesus, they will live in God's way and make the world and people happier, more peaceful and more just. Catholics believe that the moral teachings of the Church help them to know and follow the example and teaching of Jesus.

What would taking responsibility for your self involve?

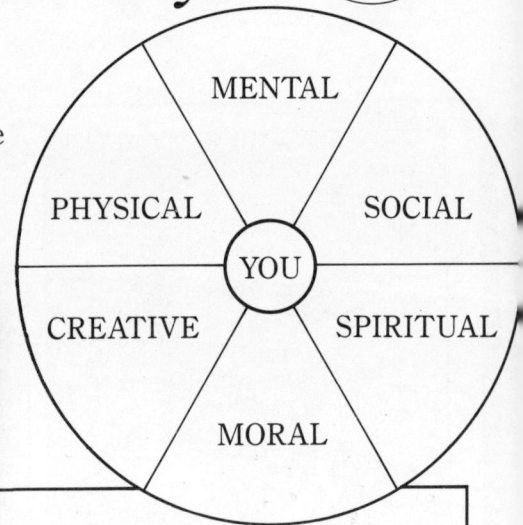

Task 17

Make a check-list of what responsibility for self might involve under the headings given. The first one has been partly done, but you might wish to add to it or to disagree with what is there.

1. PHYSICAL SELF
● Looking after your health.
● Paying attention to personal hygiene.
● Caring for your appearance.
● Taking appropriate exercise.
● Having enough rest and sleep.
● ....

2. MENTAL SELF (your knowledge, understanding, learning, emotions.)
● ....
● ....

3. SOCIAL SELF (your friendships and relationships, working with other people, etc.)
● ....
● ....

4. CREATIVE SELF (your use of your talents and time in an imaginative way.)
● ....
● ....

5. MORAL SELF (your choices and decisions about right and wrong.)
● ....
● ....

6. SPIRITUAL SELF (your attention to the deepest values in life.)
● ....
● ....

Here is a pool of words/ideas which may help you to think about this, but you may add your own words/ideas.

friendships	conscience	learning	reading
choices	values	knowledge	prayer
hobbies	expression	understanding	worship
interests	communication	peace and quiet	attitudes
relationships	language	time for reflection	being fair and just
groups to belong to	imagination	study	

Can you think of any examples or teachings of Jesus which are specially concerned with any of these aspects of personality?

Extension work

A

Which of these six aspects of personality do you think should be given most attention by:
(a) an athlete?
(b) a pupil in school?
(c) a parent?
. . . or do you think they are all equally important?

Reflect

B

Which of these six aspects of personality do you feel particularly confident about? *Why?*

Christian responsibility: responsiblity for others

Who cares?

CHARITY BEGINS AT HOME

Look after number 1 and let everyone else look after themselves.

I don't depend on anyone, so why should anyone depend on me?

Task 18 GROUP WORK

Discuss the opinions expressed by the characters above.

Analyse the consequences of working exclusively on these principles. (What sort of world would result if everyone thought this way?)

Reflect on possible responses to these views. (What reasons might there be for caring for other people and not just yourself or your closest friends and relatives?)

Explore the response of Jesus to the needs of other people. Look at the Gospel accounts of what he did:
- For a blind man
  Mark: 10:46–52.

- For a crippled woman
  Luke 13:10–13.
- For the ten people who suffered from a skin disease
  Luke 17:11–19.
- For the man with a paralysed hand
  Matthew 12:10–13.
- For the man with a physical and mental disorder
  Matthew 12:22.
- For Jairus' daughter
  Mark 5:22–24, 35–43.
- For Zacchaeus
  Luke 19:1–10.
- For the man who was crucified with him.
  Luke 23:39–42.

What he said in the stories about the:
- Good Samaritan
  Luke 10:30–37.
- Friend in need
  Luke 11:5–8.
- Lost Sheep
  Matthew 18:12–13.
- Rich man and Lazarus
  Luke 16:19–31.
- Great Commandment
  Luke: 10:25–28.

Summarize (in a couple of sentences) what you think Jesus' response would be to the characters in the drawing.

Reflect

Reflect

What evidence is there that Christian communities take seriously the idea that to be a Christian means to take responsibility for others, particularly the poor, the sick, the needy and the dying?

What have you discovered in your RE work so far that could shed light on this question?

Extension work

A

Role-play a parable or gospel incident concerned with responsibility for others.

B Drama:

Write and *present* a short dramatic scene where there is a clash of views about whether you should take responsibility for others.

Christian responsibility: stewardship of the environment

OZONE LAYER THREATENED

Acid rain kills forests | RIVERS POLLUTED

You have been considering what taking responsibility for yourself and for others might mean, and why these are central concerns in the Christian community and in most of the world faiths.

But what about the world itself – the surroundings in which you live out your life. Should you care for that?

Task 19 A class project: –

the world on trial.

The members of the class should be divided into three groups for this activity.

Group One: Collect Evidence of Pollution and Abuse of the Environment by countries, industries and individuals. Concentrate on the GLOBAL level.

Group Two: Collect Evidence of Positive Steps being taken to protect and promote a healthy and balanced environment. Concentrate on GLOBAL issues such as attempts to save the rain forests, the ozone layer, and so on.

Group Three: Decide HOW you will evaluate the evidence on both sides and then come to a JUDGEMENT about whether, in general, we are preserving or destroying the environment worldwide.

FOLLOW-UP WORK

Christian groups, like many other world faith communities and indeed political and environmental groups, believe that responsibility must be taken for the environment, the physical world and its resources.

The **motives** for holding this belief may differ in various groups.

The main reason why Christians believe that people should take responsibility for their environment is their belief that God has created it. They believe that people have been given the power to harness the rich resources of the world for the benefit of all who live here. Like a school caretaker who has the responsibility for helping the school community to look after its working environment, Christians believe that people are STEWARDS or caretakers of the world and will be held to account and judged by God for their treatment and use of the world's resources.

Read for yourself:
The Creation accounts Genesis 1 and 2.
The Flood (New Creation) Story Genesis 6:8.
The world, a new creation in Jesus
 Colossians 1:13–20.
The last judgement parable Matthew 25:31–36.

In 1986, to mark the twenty-fifth anniversary of the World Wildlife Fund, members of five of the world's major religious traditions, Buddhism, Christianity, Hinduism, Islam and Judaism, met in the Basilica of St. Francis in Assisi, Italy, at an inter-faith ceremony to bless a declaration from each of the faiths concerning nature and conservation.

Buddhist
Buddhism is a religion of love, understanding and compassion, and committed towards the ideal of non-violence. As such, it also attaches a great importance to wild life and the protection of the environment on which every being in this world depends for survival.

Christian
In his "Canticle of Brother Sun" St. Francis called all creatures his brothers and sisters because they are God's gifts and signs of his providential and reconciling love. To God alone do they belong, to him they bear a likeness, and in his name Mother earth our sister, feeds us.

Hindu
Let us declare our determination to halt the present slide towards destruction, to rediscover the ancient tradition of reverence for all life . . . Let us recall the ancient Hindu dictum: "The Earth is our mother and we are all her children".

Muslim
We are God's stewards and agents on Earth. We are not masters of this Earth; it does not belong to us to do what we wish. It belongs to God and he has entrusted us with its safekeeping.

Jewish
Our ancestor Abraham inherited his passion for nature from Adam. The later Rabbis never forgot it. Some twenty centuries ago they told the story of two men who were out on the water in a rowboat. Suddenly, one of them started to saw under his feet. He maintained that it was his right to do whatever he wished with the place that belonged to him. The other answered him that they were in the rowboat together; the hole that he was making would sink both of them.
We are all passengers together in this same fragile and glorious world. Let us safeguard our row boats and let us row together.

What similarities do you find between the five major traditions on the issue of conservation? Make a list of the similarities and of the main points included in the extracts.

Extension work

A

Analyse the way that pupils in your school treat their environment. *Find examples* of abuse of the school building and grounds, for example, litter, graffiti, and of good practice. Are there any environmental projects in the school; groups who look after a particular suite of rooms, decorative displays and so on?

Interview the caretaker or schoolkeeper and find out what he or she thinks about this.

B

Apply the approaches in Extension A to your local community (your street, parks, amenities, precinct, and so on).

71

Power and authority in Christianity ministry and service

Christians who have special responsibilities in the Church are called MINISTERS – a word which literally means SERVANTS. This means that the holding of office in the Church, position or role-power, is a form of service to God and the community. Often Christians speak of a VOCATION because they believe that God calls and inspires people to take up these tasks or ministries.

In the same way, to be a Christian is not seen as belonging to an exclusive club but as taking on responsibility – being called to live in the way that Jesus did, serving God by caring for others.

Task 20

Analyse Jesus' approach to POWER as presented in the gospels.

Read: Matthew 18:1–5
"The greatest is the one who humbles himself."
Read: John 13:3–17
"I have set you an example."
Read: Luke 14:7–11
"Whoever humbles himself will be exalted."

Reflection Look through the different kinds of power in Task 10. Which of these is closest to the kind of power which Jesus was speaking about in the extracts you have read, and in what he said and did in the readings you studied in Task 18.

Extension work

A

Role-play a situation where someone who appears to be weaker than everyone else in some respects proves to be stronger than them in an important way.

B

Reflect on the kind of leadership which Christian leaders in your country give, for example, the Archbishop of Canterbury, the Roman Catholic Cardinal, the Moderator of the Free Churches. *Examine* the contribution that ONE of them makes.
or
Study the life of Pope John XXIII who was greatly admired for his humble leadership and service to the Catholic church or the present Pope, John Paul II, who has travelled all over the world and has championed the cause of human rights.

ASSESS your work!

How did we do?

Tasks 17–20

1. *What different aspects of yourself do you think you might need to take responsibility for?*

2. *What do you feel about conservation issues? What did you learn about how some of the major religious traditions approach these issues?*

3. *What evidence is there for considering that caring for other people is important to Christians? Where does this concern come from, what is it based on?*

Review the module

Look at the list of activities planned for at the beginning of this module.

Read through your self-assessments after each group of tasks.

How did you do? Have you completed all the work planned?

On the whole, did you enjoy doing the work in this module?

We are the Champions!

Managing your own learning

Were you

1. Usually on time for class/usually late for class?
2. Hardworking . . . most of the time/some of the time/not very often?
3. Able to work by yourself sometimes?
4. Able to work with others in a group?

Did you

5. Find the work very easy or very difficult?
6. Work when the teacher was busy with other people or only when the teacher was with you?
7. Cooperate with the teacher?
8. Did you follow up any of the work you did at home by reading or finding out more about any of the topics you have covered?
9. Did you do any extension/project work?

Do you

10. Find it easy to tell the teacher of any problems you had?
11. Prefer to work by yourself or with others?

Now, share what you have done with your class teacher.

Congratulations! **You have completed** *Values*, **level Two**